We Belong *to* Big Church

CARIBBEAN SOUNDINGS AND STORIES IN ANGLICANIA

KORTRIGHT DAVIS

Tellwell Talent
www.tellwell.ca

ISBN
978-0-2288-5116-5 (Hardcover)
978-0-2288-5114-1 (Paperback)
978-0-2288-5115-8 (eBook)

Dedication

This book is dedicated to all those faithful Anglicans throughout the Caribbean and North America who have journeyed with me along this pilgrimage of worship, witness, exploration, and proclamation, and who have in so many and various ways brought vision, value, and vitality to what we are called to become as followers of Jesus Christ, and warriors in the fight for freedom, justice and full humanity.

Contents

Preface

Whenever I left my home on Bishopgate Street in St. John's Antigua, to go to church, I would turn right on Popeshead Street, and then turn left on to Newgate Street. As soon as I turned on that street, there would be that majestic view of St. John's Anglican Cathedral, my church, ahead of me on the hill. It had a commanding view of the city of St. John's, with its two towering steeples, its large clock, and its loud melodious peel of bells There was also the view of its steeply rising steps leading through two huge pillars on to further graded steps towards the large west doors. This Cathedral was built in 1848 – a double structure – with stone on the exterior and wood in the interior. We grew up calling it "Big Church". For quite a long time it was the largest edifice on the Island of Antigua. It remains the Mother Church in the Diocese of the North Eastern Caribbean and Aruba (NECA), formerly known as the Diocese of Antigua.

This is the church where I was baptized and confirmed, and where I grew up through the ranks of acolytes (or servers as we were called), and the boys' choir. Later, as a student in training for the priesthood I would occasionally perform the duties as Sub-deacon as well. It was on the steps leading into the Sanctuary of the High Altar where I was ordained to the Diaconate in December 1965. There was always a very vibrant and lively community of boys and girls, men and women, who lived in and around the City, and whose social and cultural matrix was in large measure influenced by the fact that we all belonged to "Big Church".

Of course, there were other churches in the City – Ebenezer Methodist, Spring Gardens Moravian, St. Joseph's Roman Catholic,

St. John's Seventh Day Adventist (just outside the west walls of the Cathedral), the Pilgrim Holiness Church (on Bishopgate Street, opposite my home), and the Salvation Army. Each denomination had its own climate, culture, and customs; but the one thing that we all had in common was that we referred to the Cathedral as "Big Church", whether we were members or not. "Big Church" rang out the hours from its huge clock, just as Big Ben would do in London, England; and after the chimes were added, a rich variety of hymn tunes would fill the air with sounds of joy and inspiration. It was always a local cultural treat to listen to Big Ben chiming the hours via the BBC radio broadcast while "Big Church" was chiming the hour on the hour almost at the same time, with a four hour difference by Greenwich Mean Time.

"Big Church" was therefore a sacred sanctuary for hundreds of members, as well as an architectural symbol of the majesty of God, and the source of global solidarity with the rest of the Anglican Communion. Although the genre of Anglicanism subsists in churches being in communion with the Archbishop of Canterbury, as the *primus inter pares* (first among equals), the texture of Anglicanism is as varied as the broad cultural and contextual realities of each Anglican province throughout the world. This means that, apart from the universal adherence to the So-called Chicago-Lambeth Quadrilateral (Bible, Creeds, Sacraments of Baptism and Communion, and Historic Episcopate), local varieties obtain throughout this world-wide big church fellowship.

The Anglican Communion is the third largest grouping of Christians after the Roman Catholics and the Orthodox. So, "Big Church" for us is the source and seed of membership and affiliation in the Bigger Church. This book is therefore about a range of stories and soundings relating to Anglicanism in the Caribbean, from the Caribbean, and in the Caribbean Diaspora in North America. The Anglican Church in the USA is called the Protestant Episcopal Church in the USA (PECUSA), while the Anglican Church of Canada is self-explanatory (ACC), and the Church in the Province of the West Indies (CPWI) also speaks for itself.

We Belong To Big Church is a compendium of writings, stories, and presentations that are all focused on a range of aspects and dimensions that attempt to depict a kaleidoscope of Anglicanism in general, and Afro-Anglicanism in particular. Some of the text is written in a fictional narrative style, with a strong backdrop of religious, liturgical, and ecclesiastical cultures in the Caribbean and North America. The book comprises of four sections.

The First Section is a fictional narrative depicting a woman who had migrated from an Island in the Caribbean in the late 1970's or early 1980's, having left behind one world of church life and culture. She is faced with the challenge that most immigrants from the Caribbean encounter when they have to make determined efforts to settle into a new way of life, and a faster pace here in America. The formative years of her early upbringing are a basic backdrop for her attempts to settle in with all the necessary mental, emotional, social and cultural adjustments that America demands of her. She finds a sort of new home-base, a home away from home, in the church environment, and this provides for her both solace and solidarity, proximate continuity with her native land, as well as a sphere safe enough to raise her two children in the "fear and nurture of the Lord".

The American brand of Anglicanism poses its own challenges for her, having been brought up in Caribbean Anglicanism. Nevertheless, she is determined to make as many adjustments as are necessary, for she is well aware that *"when in Rome, you have to do what the Romans do!"* The story revolves around her earnest efforts and desire to be on time for the church service one Sunday morning; hence the title of this Section is: *"Don't Be Late For Church"*. The narrative is written in an anonymizing idiom, which means that the main characters of the plot are deliberately left nameless, in the hope that readers might find it coincidental to be identified in some way with any one of them.

I had in mind the literary device that is used in the Fourth Gospel in the New Testament, where the writer of that sacred text refers quite often to "the disciple whom Jesus loved", without giving him a name. I really have no argument with those who insist that his name was "John". I simply affirm that the Gospel text does not actually say so, even though the John 21:24 attribution of authorship comes fairly close to lifting the anonymity! The lady and her whole family shall remain nameless, just as much as the Island where she was born and grew up before coming to America. She is an Afro-Anglican in the Episcopal Church here in America and she simply yearns to be early for church on this special Sunday.

The Second Section is also a fictional narrative, and this time most of the characters are given names. The script is entitled *"Cleibert Bynoe's Pilgrimage"*. The plot is an informational tour of various Afro-Anglican congregations in the Episcopal Church alongside some of the specific ministries, programs and institutional structures that relate to the membership of Blacks in a predominantly White Church. Cleibert Bynoe is a Barbadian Anglican who has grown up in the church, with a lively participation in almost every aspect of ministry in that religious community. In spite of the historical legacies of plantation slavery, racism, classism, and colonialism (both ecclesiastical and governmental), Anglicanism in Barbados has been mainly a Black religious social and cultural expression.

Cleibert Bynoe was birthed, baptized, confirmed, and reared in the full crucibles of the Black Anglican experience, allied with some steady linkages and legacies of things originally British, whether it was in music, ritual, liturgy or church order. The historical connections between the Church of England and its missionary societies reach back into the seventeenth century. The Bishop of London was responsible for the churches in Barbados until 1824 when the Diocese of Barbados was established along with the Diocese of Jamaica. Church architecture, place names, and some public monuments all give meaning to the reason why Barbados has been traditionally nicknamed "Little England". Barbadian Anglicanism has managed to retain some of these historical and cultural vestiges, while it forges a novel path towards authentic indigenization and contextual efficacy.

Barbadians have been migrating to America for several generations now, and they have been able to establish themselves in many areas of professional, educational, political, industrial, and religious endeavor. Just as our African ancestors had brought their religious endowments with them across the Middle Passage, so had Barbadians taken their ecclesial cultural habits with them across the Atlantic as they settled in

America. For the most part, they would have joined themselves to some established religious denominations, or else they would have founded their own congregations over time to guarantee their own religious and institutional autonomy. Generations of them, however, would strive to remain Anglican in America, making strenuous efforts to find ecclesiastical accommodation and relative comfort in the strangely lukewarm climate of the Episcopal Church.

Barbadians therefore have always formed a significant section of the mosaic of Afro-Anglicanism in the Episcopal Church, with several clergymen migrating as well to find greener pastures, and some lay-persons eventually being ordained into the priesthood. It is not without merit to record that the first Barbadian to be consecrated a Bishop in the Episcopal Church has been Bishop Deon Johnson of Missouri. He was recently enthroned in the summer of 2020. Indeed, the cultural and historical linkages between Anglicanism in Barbados and Afro-Anglicanism in America are so strong that when the Planning Committee for the first Afro-Anglican Conference was setting its plans in order, the only location considered for this historic event was Barbados.

The evolution of the Planning Committee and its proceedings are a historic narrative, especially as it involved the active participation of representatives from all sectors of Afro-Anglicanism throughout the Communion. More particularly, however, the historical significance of Codrington College in Barbados was a major drawing card, since the history of the College and the legacy surrounding its establishment provided an important backdrop for what the Conference was being designed to explore and promote. What does it mean to be Black and Anglican at the same time? What are the distinguishing characteristics of Black Anglicanism? How would the Anglican Communion reconfigure itself to take into full account the global demographics of its total membership? How would the historical vestiges of British imperialism be systematically and theologically expunged from the modern face of Anglicanism? These and other pertinent and pressing questions would engage the assembly of Anglicans from around the world for a week of deliberations and celebrations.

The original decision was to name the conference the "Conference of Black Episcopalians". This was mainly since the idea of the meeting was generated by a group of Black Episcopalians in America, who were always very conscious of the fact that they were a minority sector in a predominantly White Church. Accordingly, they were mainly active in acquiring a greater level of participation and in the decision-making and leadership councils of the church. At the same time, they were conscious of the fact that the global Anglican Communion was predominantly non-White. The issue then revolved around the naming of the Inaugural Conference with a designation ("Black Episcopalians") that did not make much sense in Barbados, where Anglicanism was essentially a Black cultural and religious social expression. The Planners therefore agreed to accept my suggestion that the term "Afro-Anglican" should be introduced and promulgated.

Thus, in 1985, the First Afro-Anglican Conference was convened in Barbados, at which broad definitional and descriptive approaches to the inter-cultural and contextual realities of Afro-Anglicanism were widely discussed. The historic document known as "The Codrington Consensus" emerged as an initial defining agreement on what would be projected and promulgated as major themes and fresh ways of Anglican engagement by people of color, as members of the world-wide Anglican Communion. The Codrington Consensus took on a life of its own after the Barbados assembly, and it formed the basis for further Afro-Anglican collaboration at Cambridge University in a Pre-Lambeth gathering which produced the historic "Cambridge Declaration" in 1988. It is important that this year was the ten-year meeting for all Bishops in the entire Anglican Communion, and most of these bishops were people of color. Both documents eventually contributed to some aspects of debate among the bishops at the 1988 Lambeth Conference, where some determinations clearly indicated that Afro-Anglicanism had already become a vital force to be recognized and acknowledged throughout the Anglican Communion.

All of this had its formative origins in Barbados from where our character Cleibert Bynoe would set out on his pilgrimage to explore and experience some of the life and character of Black participation in the Episcopal Church here in America. This would become for Cleibert Bynoe an exciting and illuminating survey of what it meant to be a member of "Big Church". As he travelled among the various congregations, observing their ways and interacting with their leaders, it would impress on him even more profoundly what he meant whenever he said to himself, *"We Belong To Big Church"*. This Second Section then, is an imaginative excursion amongst various types of congregations and churches that are mainly comprised of Afro-Anglicans, whether native or immigrant. The encounters which Cleibert is made to engage in throughout his visits will have provided him with a lively and comprehensive assessment of Anglicanism both at home (Barbados) and abroad (America).

The Third Section is entitled *"Soundings In Caribbean Anglicania"*. It is comprised of a series of sermons and presentations which I was privileged to be invited to deliver in various Diocesan gatherings throughout the CPWI. These invitations always meant a lot to me, if for no other reason that it afforded me many opportunities to make some small contributions to the theological and pastoral life of the Church in the region from which I had come. I have always been mindful of the enormous debt of gratitude for so much of my early formation as a priest and scholar. This sense of indebtedness has been matched by a strong sense of obligation to continue my active participation in the growth and development of opportunities for ministry and witness throughout the Caribbean Church. That Church has poured so much into my own journey of priestly vocation and theological career both at Codrington College (as student and teacher), and at Howard University School of Divinity as a member of its faculty. Traversing the CPWI Dioceses, then, except the Dioceses of Belize and Guyana, has undoubtedly enriched my own sense of "Belonging To Big Church". It has afforded me some invaluable experiences of ecclesial fellowship and missional solidarity, all in the joy of the Gospel of Jesus Christ.

The Fourth Section chronicles the texts of two historic lectures in the Anglican Church of Canada, where the challenges of dealing with Racism, Multiculturalism, and inclusion of First Nation Christians have been present for generations. The efforts of Trinity College, Toronto to address these issues have historically taken many forms. The Romney Moseley Lecture series was inaugurated to serve as one such effort. They were named in honor of The Reverend Dr. Romney Moseley who was a Professor of Ethics at Trinity College, a Barbadian scholar who was also an Anglican priest. He died suddenly in Toronto while celebrating the Eucharist at a downtown church one Sunday morning. His efforts to deal with the racial and cultural challenges were highly thought of, and his legacy was quite pivotal in some of the programs that followed his demise. Chief among them has been the "Black Anglicans Of Canada", an organization that may well be regarded as the Canadian counterpart to the "Union Of Black Episcopalians" (UBE) in the Episcopal Church.

It is my fervent hope that this volume will serve to stimulate some further conversations in Ecclesia Anglicana both in North America and the Caribbean, especially with respect to the cross-cultural, inter-cultural, and multicultural obligations and ministries within the wider church. In the final analysis, the core of the Anglican Communion subsists in its ability to promote and sustain a high level of what are known as the "Bonds Of Affection", as well as the implications and imperatives that are inherent in the Anglican ethos of MRI, that is, Mutual Respect and Interdependence.

Kortright Davis
Kensington, Maryland, November 2020

Section One

Don't Be Late For Church

I

—

She was hoping to be early for church this Sunday morning, for it was to be some special festival day. Her church was always having some festival of one kind or another. Church people had a way of wanting to celebrate their favorite seasons. These could be Harvest, Independence celebrations for many nationalities, Fathers' day, Mothers' day, Education Sunday, Homecoming, or even the Rector's anniversary. Sometimes the different church organizations wanted to hold some special Sunday events in order to invite their friends and relatives who were not members of the church. This would always give them an opportunity to dress up, stand up, speak up, and show off.

But since they did not have any other place in the community for them to be seen, and heard, and taken seriously, church provided a good space for most of the members. And, since they worked so hard in the kitchen Sunday after Sunday, and in the church garden when called upon to help, there was every reason why they should have their turn in church to be on prominent display.

There was going to be some church festival this Sunday, but she could not remember which one it was, or what exactly it was to be all about. She had not seen a church bulletin for last Sunday because she was absent from church. Many members had a way of leaving the bulletins behind in the pews after the service, and therefore they could not remember from one Sunday to the other what was due to happen during the coming week. The preacher had always urged them to count their blessings; to name them one by one; and that it would surprise them what the Lord had done.

They always wanted to take that advice a little further by insisting on counting their surprises as well, and to name them two by two. That was why they preferred to afford themselves a certain element of surprise in going to church without knowing what to expect. It was different, of course, when they had to be involved in some special part of the worship service, or with some duties in the kitchen and fellowship hall downstairs. They would read the bulletin while the minister was in the pulpit preaching his head off, and sometimes his heart out. They would check on some of the advertisements and notices that filled up so much space in the bulletins. Advertisements were an important section of their bulletins because they helped to increase the revenue for the church finances.

Of course, not every kind of business could be advertised in church; even though, as far as she was concerned, some of those advertisements really crossed the line. Political meetings, Saturday night dances sponsored by restaurant owners, trips to gambling casinos, or shop sales, all seemed to her to be unacceptable. After all, in church literature that was promoting the Word of God, and inspiring people to live decent and holy lives by the Worship of God, there should be no place for such worldly endeavors. But the church needed the money to maintain its mission and to promote the Work of God. They had often heard preachers suggest that, in the mission of the church, Word, Worship, and Work went together, and that money was essential for such ministries.

Most of the members seemed to hold to the view that even money donated to the church from questionable sources could become useful, as long as it was blessed before being used. Some even argued that not all the money dropped in the collection bags had come from "clean" sources, but as long as it was to be used for the work of the Lord, and in the house of the Lord, God would not only understand, but God would also forgive whatever sins were done unwittingly. It was sometimes suspected that some of the large donations that reached into the church coffers had indeed come from shady deals with special intentions of expressing gratitude to God for good luck, or favorable escapes from detection and detention. The well-known rule of "Don't ask and don't tell" was sometimes observed when unusual donations reached the church. But that was another matter around which most members preferred to remain silent.

People had their misgivings, but they did not earn enough money to compensate for the prohibition of 'secular' advertisements in 'sacred' literature. They just generally decided to say nothing and leave those bulletins in church as they returned to their homes. They would pay attention to who were celebrating birthdays and anniversaries that coming week, or during the current month. Many of the announcements virtually went in through the eyes and then out through the ears. But, other than that, not many of the members deemed the bulletins worth taking home. That would only increase the volume of paper in their own houses with which they had to contend. She was prepared to content herself with the fact if she didn't have access to the bulletin from the last Sunday, she could not know what was coming up this Sunday. She was going to church, and she didn't want to be late today.

It was to be a day of celebration, and the Rector just loved to give them what they wanted. It made him feel that he was ministering to the people where they were, and that he was responding to their needs adequately and lovingly. He loved the people, and the people loved him, so far. In any event, festivals were great money-making occasions, and the special envelopes would flood the pews and church boxes in search of more dollars for the church's programs. Since her church-members did not believe in second collections at the end of the services, like those Baptist people, and the Pentecostals, they had to arrange for special envelopes for special occasions. Now and again, the church would insist that members should march up to the altar rail, where some of the ushers were standing with deep baskets, and then deposit their special offerings. Some members objected strongly to this strategic ritual, since, in their opinion, it showed up those who had to give and those who didn't have anything to give. It was for them an instant display of "the haves and the have-nots". This seemed to them to be a violation of the Christian principle of all persons being equal in the sight of God, and especially in the house of God. The church really needed to promote extra fund-raisers, but some efforts made for some congregational discomforts. It was a persistent moral and pastoral dilemma for the church.

As a matter of fact, many of those people in her church had left the Baptists, Church of God, Pentecostal, or other such denominations, in order to escape the "tyranny" of the multiple collections during the same service. Many of them called it 'tyranny' mainly because of the high-pitch way in which the deacons, and trustees, and pastors would try to make them feel guilty if they couldn't donate. Quite often they would hear repeatedly that God favored those who were generous, but that God frowned on those who grumbled as they gave. They had seen themselves as economic church refugees, running from the high cost of church giving to enjoy a lower cost of high church living.

Yet she was not one of them, for she had been an Anglican all her life, just as her mother and grandmother, and great grandmother. Festivals were plentiful, but collections were not. The church people only had to take care of business with the special envelopes from time to time. Despite the envelopes, they thought, it was still cheaper to be an Anglican than to be a Baptist, as far as the cost of giving was concerned, even if the Anglican services were not entirely to their cultural liking, or emotional satisfaction.

Now it was not that the Rector really loved the money, for he was always in a habit of reminding his members that the love of money was the root of all evil, according to the Bible. But, most of the time, he came close to sounding like if he really had a strong love for the money himself, and that more festivals in the church would bring in more money for the church. The more the merrier, he often seemed to say. Festivals and big collections went together. But festivals and plenty people also went together. If you did not get to church early, you would not get a good seat. She really wanted to be early this morning.

One of her good friends had phoned to tell her what had gone on in church last Sunday. She heard who had preached, but the sermon was not all that exciting, or even worth remembering. It was a sermon about Job. The preacher had told them a joke about a country minister and a man in an African village. The story went like this. *One day a minister was walking through the village when he saw a young man carrying a goat on his head back to the animal pen nearby. All of a sudden, the young man seemed to have gotten angry with the goat, and he threw it down on the ground with a passion and started to beat the animal. The minster quickly ran to the goat's defense and to chastise the young man for his blatant cruelty. The minister said: "Oh no! No! No! Young man; that's not the way to treat an innocent animal! They are also creatures of God. You must have more patience like Job." The young man replied instantly: "Parson, you can say whatever you like. But let me tell you something. No goat ever soiled Job's head!" Leaving the goat to its own predicament, the minister calmly walked on, as if theologically defeated.*

She heard about who had read the lessons; and who had been celebrating anniversaries and so on. But she could not remember if her friend had told her exactly what this festival was all about. After all, a whole week had passed, and so much else had happened during the week. Church news virtually faded by Sunday nights, for Monday mornings would always bring their own trials and frustrations.

Why had she missed church last Sunday? It really was not so much that she had missed, but that the time just missed her, and she was not able to get the children together and ready in time. But why did the time miss her? It was because she had been in one big argument with her husband early that morning, and by the time she had cooled down all the buses had already passed. Life was not that easy at home, and church always gave her a bit of relief from the struggles and tensions of a Saturday night or a Sunday morning – the children one way, and her husband another.

When it came to her husband, however, he wasn't into much of this "church thing" at all. As a matter of fact, he often told her that he could not bring himself to go to any church in this country, for, as far as he was concerned, the ministers were a bunch of so-and-so's. They loved too much money. They loved too many women. Some of them had interfered with the little boys and had even driven some of the boys to drink and drugs. Most of them couldn't preach like his favorite parsons back home. He did not feel that church was for hard-working men like him. He had to maintain two jobs in order to put food on the table

7

and send money back home for his old auntie and her spinster sister. But that was not all.

"Wha' you get out o' all dat church stuff?" He would often ask her. "You tink you better than anybody else?"

Old people back home used to tell him, "nearer to church farther from God", and he often found that to be quite true. Take for instance Mr. Sampson the shopkeeper back home in Mason Village. In his opinion, Mr. Sampson was one of the biggest crooks the world had ever known. He had grown to believe that all shopkeepers were going to hell, because they had already sold their souls to the Devil by all their crooked deals. But Mr. Sampson was one of the leading members of the local Village church. He was always picking up the collection, or reading the lessons, or singing louder than anybody else in the Sunday services. He would even attempt to direct the choir when, in his considered opinion, the organist wanted a little help. Now remember, Mr. Sampson did not know how to read even one note of music!

One day when Mr. Sampson was taking an order of milk from the milk-woman, her husband was in the shop buying some cornmeal and red herring for his mother's special menu. He was about fifteen years old at the time. He watched Mr. Sampson bring in the pail of milk from the milk-woman, pour some of the milk in four rum bottles up to about three-quarters, and then fill the rest of the bottles with water. Mr. Sampson made sure that he stretched the milk so far that it would be soapy, soapy, when you rubbed a little drop of it in your hand.

Neither did Mr. Sampson agree with the old arithmetic that sixteen ounces made one pound. He used to hide the scales behind a special piece of cardboard just below the counter so that people could not see what he was weighing. Whenever you called for a pound of cornmeal, or rice, or sugar, or even a pound of salt-fish, he made sure that you only got fourteen ounces. Once when the trade inspector caught him doing it to a customer, Mr. Sampson argued that the scale was not balancing properly, and that the "fourteen" was really a "sixteen". But there was really nothing wrong with Sampson's scale. He was just a thief in the shop, and still a chief in the church. But, guess what; he was not the only one!

Miss Brathwaite was another one, he remembered. She used to sell fruit and vegetables by the main road, not far from Sampson's shop. Sampson made sure that she did not sell right in front of his shop, because she had a big mouth, and a very loud voice, and she would often harass the people who went in to buy from him. Among the many things that Sampson disliked about her was the fact that she never seemed to be properly dressed, or to be sitting like a lady beside her trays of produce. Although they both belonged to the same church, they would always be in ding-dong arguments over who was more of a thief than who, and who was robbing whom out of their rightful and loyal customers. Miss Brathwaite would try to undercut Sampson's sales with some sweets, and sugar-cakes, and slice-ups (made from coconut and sugar), and peanut candy, and fudge, and chocolates, and delicacies like that.

The sun would often melt Brathwaite's goods in the tray; not to talk about the flies that she had to keep brushing away morning, noon and night, especially if she stayed out long after the sun had gone down. Yes indeed, she was a businesswoman in her own right, and a churchwoman to her own delight. She was not as high up in the church as Sampson, but she could hold her own quite well, and she made sure that she would not be left out of whatever was going on in the church. But she was just as "scampish" as Sampson in her trading deals. So, as far as he was concerned, not only shopkeepers, but hucksters as well, were all going to hell. That was why he had developed very little use for the church, ever since he was back home. Coming to America did not help to change his opinions. In fact, there was enough to justify his disdain for organized religion in this country, even though he did nothing to stand in the way of his wife and children being actively involved in their church life.

But truth be told, he was not always like that. Growing up in Mason Village he had been a regular churchgoer. His mother made sure that he was regular at church whether he wanted to go or not. Sunday School, Cub-scouts, Junior Choir, and Boys Brigade were all part of his upbringing, especially as they all provided an opportunity to dress in special uniforms. Church-related uniforms were very different from home-clothes, school-clothes, or yard-clothes when he had to work in the garden or carry water from the Village cistern. He used to take to all these organizations like a fish takes to water. But all that was then. Now that he was in America, it was a different story altogether. The only religious theme that kept him self-satisfied was that part of Scripture which said that the non-church-going husband was sanctified in the church-going wife. That was enough for him. Nobody could get him into any church, unless on very rare occasions, or for special events involving his family.

But her attitude to church back home and her experiences with church people in her village were not as negative as her husband's. She relished the many ways in which her encounters and association with the leaders of her church had made an indelible impression on her character, her upbringing, and her general attitude to life itself. For just as often as her husband would bring up stories about Mr. Sampson's character in his church, or Miss Brathwaite's conspicuous manners at her trading spot, she found it necessary to counter with some pleasant memories and impressions of her own out of her church community.

They had both come from the same Island, but they had grown up in different villages. They had only met and fell in love after they were in America. The courtship and engagement had not been very long either, for they had both agreed very early on in the relationship that partnership and shared livelihood, in a stable and loving marriage, made more sense than any prolonged living apart from each other. While it is often said that opposites attract, they were quite content to embrace two slightly differing approaches to the practice of their religion, if it would not redound to the detriment of the children's proper growth and character development. She was church-allied, but he was church-allergic.

Whether it was in the Sunday School, or the Girl's Brigade, or even the Flower Group, her dealings with church members always left her with a sense of worth and well-being. The elders of the church were often very careful to ensure that they proffered good advice and showered her with lessons for growing into full adulthood as a decent and respectable young lady. Two persons stood out in her memory. They had made an indelible impression on her understanding of good character and human dignity, both in the church and in the village community. One was her Sunday School teacher "Aunt Mavis" (her real name was Mavis Hunte). Aunt Mavis was not really her aunt, but it was a term of endearment and respect that all the children and young adults used to address her. Aunt Mavis had no children of her own. The other was "Teacher Joe" (his real name was Joseph Maynes). He was not a professional teacher, but he served as a Lay-reader and Catechist, mainly in preparing candidates for Confirmation. That earned him the right to be addressed as "Teacher" as simply a mark of respect and recognized authority both within the church and beyond.

Aunt Mavis was a seamstress. She would specialize in making sure that all the little girls in the village were properly dressed, and beautifully adorned for church services. Of course, there were so many families that she sewed for that there was often a competition as to whose outfits looked the smartest. This competition was especially fierce at three seasons of the year – Christmas, Easter, and Harvest. Not only was it regarded as a "no-no" to wear the same outfit twice; it was also frowned upon if any two girls seemed to have been dressed alike when they were not from the same family. If they were from the same family, then a certain level of hand-me-downs was acceptable for the younger girls, but not teenagers. But then, the younger sisters were not particularly pleased to show up at church festivals wearing outfits that had been seen on older siblings on previous occasions. Church festivals were essentially fashion parades in themselves, and Aunt Mavis featured in the middle of it all, not only for good business, but also for careful designing and prominence in the village as an accomplished and upstanding church-lady.

She held Aunt Mavis in high regard, not just because she was the best seamstress in the village, nor because she always looked out for her on her way to and from school. Aunt Mavis was special to her because she exuded that character of dignity, decency, and discipline which made itself most obvious in her role as a Sunday School teacher. Sunday School classes were mixed in gender, with boys and girls of the same ages huddled together to learn about God and the life of Jesus. It took a great deal of tact and vigilance to ensure that the boys behaved themselves in the company of the girls – no teasing, no pinching, no unseemly remarks, and no fidgeting. Aunt Mavis was for her the genuine embodiment of compassion, competence, and consequence – consequence in the sense that she was somebody who could be a role model in church and community.

That was why she not only held her in very high regard but held on to her as a mentor and civic exemplar as she herself grew into maturity, and as she migrated to America with that strong sense of purpose and personhood. Quite often, as she faced some challenging circumstances early in her sojourn in this strange and diverse society, she would often ask herself how would Aunt Mavis deal with such and such an issue? This kept her wedded to church life. This kept her wedded to her husband and her three children – two girls and a boy. This kept her struggling to set her priorities in the right order, for that was what she had learned in Sunday School back home. Aunt Mavis would often teach them some memory verses from the Scriptures; and most of them were etched in her memory. She never bothered to ask herself what was meant by these verses, except to console herself that the trials and anxieties of navigating life through family, church, and society could not overwhelm God's sufficiency of grace in her life. So, church meant a lot to her, and on the mental strength of her parents and Aunt Mavis, she was travelling along life's pathway. She often recalled one important verse that she had learned in Sunday School which said that loving and living go together with learning.

Teacher Joe also contributed to her spiritual growth and social well-being; but not as much as Aunt Mavis. Teacher Joe was a gentle soul. He was always finding a good word to say to others, and about others. He seemed never to miss a chance to offer good advice to those who sought his counsel. He found himself often repeating a mantra that he himself had learned as a boy in school – *Manners maketh man*. In fact, Teacher Joe was a walking anthology of proverbs, aphorisms, folk sayings, and Biblical texts that he had memorized over the years. His grandmother had often repeated many of them in his presence in the hope that he would hear them, learn them, repeat them, and live by them. Especially when he was training his candidates for Confirmation, he would always insist that they repeated them systematically and poetically if possible, so that they would stick in their young and tender psyches for a lifetime. She particularly remembered Teacher Joe drilling into them this saying – *Give unto others the best you have and the best will come back to you.*

Of course, not all the sayings from Teacher Joe made her very comfortable, if only for the fact that they sounded somewhat complex to her young and growing mind. One such saying was scriptural that referred to casting bread on water and finding it after a long time. She could not really comprehend why people would want to throw away good bread, especially when there was an occasional scarcity of that staple food. Bread was made from flour. The flour had to be imported from North America. Bakers had to spend a lot of time in the areas of the hot ovens, staying up all night so that people could buy hot fresh bread in the mornings. Nobody liked to buy stale bread. Stale bread was still useful though, for her family would feed the fowls and the pigs with it along with some other food items that were no longer fit for human consumption. So, there was really no point in throwing away good bread, and certainly not into the sea, or into the streams that ran into the creeks not far from her home.

It was only after she had grown into full womanhood and was now living in America by this time, that she was able to associate what she had learned from Teacher Joe with what she was hearing in church. By that time, she was able to experience many "eureka" moments in church by associating some new religious and moral sayings with what Teacher Joe's sayings must have meant. His moral seedlings were at last beginning to germinate and to bear fruit in her ways of life here in America. It was now possible for her to link that complex saying about the bread with another scriptural saying that the preacher was fond of repeating that people often reaped what they themselves had sown.

One of her Trinidadian friends would often exclaim that *"Cow don' mek sheep"*. Her Grenadian colleague who worked in the same establishment had a way of reminding her that *You can't get guavas from a nutmeg tree.* She had a friend from Montserrat who often used a different kind of folk saying that she loved. It said: *"What is joke for one is death for another!"* On the whole, Caribbean folk wisdom was fully laden with sayings cultural, proverbial, and scriptural It was virtually impossible for anyone growing up in the region to be unaccustomed to being drilled with a copious supply of them, whether they liked it or not. Teacher Joe had obviously laid a good foundation for her, and his leadership and guidance contributed enormously to her loyalty to God, her commitment to church-life, and her determination to be the best possible wife and mother.

II
———

She was still trying her very best to be early today, for she wanted to sit in a certain pew higher up in the church. The last Sunday that she was in church she was very late, and she had to sit in the back. She did not like sitting in those back pews at all, because there was always so much noise coming from the street outside. Car horns would be blazing with some fancy melodies to attract attention to other drivers. Very loud name-calling, as if to wake the dead to life again, was a constant source of annoyance. Japanese-made boom-boxes, turned up to their loudest as if to outdo any possible peels of thunder. These were usually operated by those people from the West Indies, or "the Islands" (as the Americans would say), who could not speak a word of Japanese. Defective automobile mufflers were always trying to make their own street music. Even the occasional quarrels by the street people to settle debts gone bad, or junkies gone mad, would saturate the environment outside the church.

It was certainly not like back home where there were not that many cars, and where radios in those days were mainly kept in the houses. The only times they would be carried on the streets was during the cricket season when the West Indies team was playing in a test match. It was as if the whole Island had to know the score after every ball was bowled. In cricket, six balls bowled from one wicket to the other wicket comprised an "over". Usually, the radio commentators would give the latest score after each over, except when the batsman had hit a four or a six. But the people in the Islands had often complained to the owners of the radio stations that their commentators were no good.

They complained that the commentators kept the score to themselves for too long and had no consideration for the people away from the cricket grounds. After all, whether they were working, washing, or just walking, the public had to depend on the radio commentary for the latest score. Every good cricket commentator therefore knew that he had to give the latest score after every ball was bowled, or else that would be the end of him and cricket commentary. That was why radios went everywhere during the cricket season. Otherwise, they were kept safely at home, out of the range of being a social nuisance.

Back in the Islands, the churches were usually a good way in from the streets, and you had to walk through the burial-ground to get to the church building. It was as if all those duppies in the tombs were watching what you were wearing. Duppies had nothing else to do for the rest of the time but to mind the business of those who were still alive, she used to think. America did not seem to have any duppies. Or, at the very least, she never heard anybody talking about them.

Here in America, the church was right on the street, and the people in the neighborhood made so much noise in its vicinity. The doors and windows were supposed to be shut for the sake of the air-conditioner with its stale air, or the heater with its stuffy air during the cold days. She was accustomed to fresh air back home; but here, everything was so artificial, even the church air, mixed as it was with the outside noise. She just could not concentrate very easily on her worship, but she was still glad to get to church whenever she could.

It was hard enough to concentrate on the worship with all that was going on inside the church itself. But when she had to be subjected to those major distractions and annoyances on the outside as well, it made life far more difficult for her, and for those who had assembled for worship in the house of the Lord. People just did not have as much respect for places of worship anywhere these days, she often thought. And especially when it was in their neighborhood, they seemed to reserve to themselves the right to establish their own noise levels. They could create their own commotion, regardless of whose sacred space was being invaded; or regardless of which "God" was being worshipped at the time. That was a different story. The trouble was that there were too many places of worship in America, she often thought to herself. There were too many religions, too many different claims about too many gods.

It seemed to her as if the people in the neighborhood just could not be bothered to take any of these claims seriously. They hid behind the common law of America that there was supposed to be a separation between Church and State. The streets belonged to the state, didn't they? So, the noise which she was hearing in the church, coming from the streets, was legitimate noise, and the church could not do much about it, mainly because of this separation. Separation was separation, and that was that!

Sitting in the back was always difficult for her ever since she was back home in the Islands. As a young girl she was accustomed to getting to church early and sitting in the second pew from the cross aisle. She did not live too far from the church, and she always went on ahead of the other members of her family, especially her younger brothers, who did not particularly like to go to church. They did not understand much of what the ministers were saying in the pulpit, or up there at the altar with their backs turned to the people. They always thought it was bad manners to speak to all those people with their backs turned to the people. It was always a curious sight for them to see these old White English ministers talking to the Black people or praying for them with their backs turned to them.

It always struck them as bad manners; but they never were bold enough to say so. That was because all the adults believed that, if you came from England as missionaries to the Islands, you had all the manners, the good manners, and the Island people only had some. Some ministers had even been arrogant enough to suggest that the Queen had sent them out from England to teach the Island people good manners. But talking to a crowd of people with your back turned to them was not what these little boys understood to be good manners.

Sometimes, it looked to the little boys as if the ministers turned their backs to them in order to hide what they were doing up there at the altar table. They would move their hands in some strange ways, up and down, up and down, out and in, or left and right, north and south.

It was even worse when they were trying to throw some smoke from a firepot on whatever they had on the table, but the smoke would not stick. It always blew out of the window. They called the smoke incense but, as far as they were concerned, smoke was smoke, whether it was in church, or in their own back yard kitchen, or when they were roasting corn in the gully.

Church smoke did not smell as sweet as roast corn smoke, and there was nothing to eat after the church smoke. But the smell of roast corn was always followed by the taste of roast corn. They preferred corn smoke to incense smoke any day. Sometimes the ministers would kneel and get up, kneel again as if they could not make up their minds whether they should stay down for good. Sometimes the little brothers thought that the ministers were so busy up there with their hands, mumbling something all to themselves, that they could swear that they were trying to keep some little living object from falling off the altar table. But they never saw what it was, for by the time the service was finished they would cover over whatever it was with a pretty colored cloth and take it all back into the little room behind the church.

It was all very secretive to them, so they were not very moved by the dramatics of the ministers up there. Again, the teachers in the Sunday School were too strict, and lacking in fun. Her brothers would do anything, plan any trick, or get themselves into any kind of predicament, just to stay away from going to church or Sunday School. It was worse when their mother made the big mistake of giving them money for the collection before they left home. They would think of all kinds of things to do with the few cents; for a few cents to them was a lot of money in those days. They had often heard it said that "one-by-one full basket", so one cent in the collection was enough and they would keep the rest for better and sweeter things. If they kept the collection, they would say to themselves, rather than put it all in that cloth collection-bag which the old men in the church would push up in their faces during the service at collection time; they would soon have enough to buy something nice.

Their little pennies could easily buy "slice-up", or "sugar-cake", or "coconut tart", or other kinds of candy. But they often had to hide their purchase before anybody could see them with it. They just did not care much for church, and they cared much less for getting rid of the little change which they were given by putting it all into the collection bag. Somebody said that it was stealing from God. But they often argued among themselves that God had so much money that he would not miss a little piece of change that poor little boys needed to buy something to make them happy.

They said that God wanted them to be happy; so God would hardly frown on their using their own initiative to help themselves out in their own way, with their own happiness, by spending their own collection in a nice little way. They had often overheard their parents say that God helped those who helped themselves. That was the little world in which her brothers operated. But she was different from them, and deeply religious. Getting to church on time was never a big thing for her; it became a part of her very personality. You could count on her to be early in those days. Those were the days when life was care-free, and sweet, with not too much to worry about, and nobody to look after but herself.

She always looked forward to sitting near that cross aisle so that she could get a good view of the whole church with all its comings and goings. She could see who was coming in from the North door, who was coming in from the South door, and who was bold enough to go further up beyond the cross aisle in those seats in the front. Some people used to say that those seats higher up were for the rich and powerful, but the people who usually sat up there never dressed up to look any richer than the people who sat in the back. The few rich people that she knew never looked particularly great when they dressed for church. Some of them wore clothes that looked like "han'-me-downs", or "gi'-tuh-me", as they called them in the Islands.

Some of them never looked any different from the poorer people sitting behind them. As a matter of fact, she remembered once asking her mother why it was that some rich people always looked so bad in expensive clothes. Her mother explained to her that it all depended on how people carried themselves when they were dressed up. Rich people had too much money to really worry about how they looked when they were in the company of poorer people. Their wealth would do all the talking for them. That was why the richer they got, the worse they looked. Poor people, her mother said, often had nothing else to depend on but their style and their "look-rich" behavior. That was why, in one sense, it was still true to say that some people looked rich from far, but they were far from rich.

When it came to the powerful, as far as she was concerned, the powerful people never bothered much with church. They stayed at home selling in their shops, or perhaps counting all the money they had made the night before. You only saw them at Harvest festivals, funerals, weddings, or christenings. What made them powerful was the strong influence they had on the public officials, who would often be seen hanging out with them, or chatting with their relatives. When it came to official functions, the people who got the invitations, or were asked to speak, were generally regarded as 'the powerful'. They were the ones who would get the jobs and the contracts from the government. They were the ones who would pay for the receptions and promotional materials for the politicians when election time came around. They were the ones whose relatives would get an easy time from the police or the local constables. In short, the powerful could do no wrong.

Or at least, that was how she thought when she lived in the Islands. But only recently, she had read in the newspapers that one or two of the old-time powerful people had fallen on hard times; their shops had been closed, and they were now out of favor with the public officials. They no longer had anything to give. When you have money, she said, you have many so-called friends; but when you go broke, all you' friends gon'. So, it does not always pay to be powerful. It was her Granma who used to warn people that people who kept low would not be afraid of falling.

Sometimes she was thinking that the so-called "rich and powerful" were those who wanted to think that they really were, even though they were not. The only time they felt rich or powerful was when they stepped into church for everybody else to see them stepping and strutting their stuff. But they did not have any wealth or power after all. It was the church which gave them that feeling, however false and pretentious it was. One of her friends had once drawn to her attention that the people who behaved as if they were rich and powerful in church were mainly those who did not have much power in their own homes, especially the men. So, they tended to exhibit an air of importance among the church people, especially when they could not exercise any power or control in their own homes. That suggestion seemed to her to have some merit to it, but she still could not understand why people would use the church for that kind of personal exhibition.

Some said that the higher seats should be for those who were living good and exemplary lives in the community. Some even said that they were reserved for the people who gave a lot of money every Sunday. She would often see visitors being escorted to those seats, but she could not really understand if they were special seats. Perhaps they were just seats nearer to the altar for those who could neither hear, nor see very well. It never bothered her, for she always preferred to seat herself right in that favorite pew just below the cross aisle, with the cross breeze, and the cross-roads in the church, and the parade of congregants all within her sacred but curious gaze.

From that vantage point she could check out whether that little girl for Miss Mattie was wearing the same dress she had on the week before. Had Mr. Moseley changed that awful bowtie, he could not fix properly last week? She could never understand why some old men liked to put on things which they could not fix properly, or which clearly did not suit them. But Mr. Moseley had this grandson in America who would often send him these young-looking clothes, not really fitting for his advanced years. Moseley took great pride in wearing them out every Sunday, just to make himself look younger than he really was.

She did not have much time for people who were always at great pains to fight against the age that God had given them; and Mr. Moseley appeared to her to be one such person with his crooked bowtie. After all, she used to say to herself, age was honor; and people who were privileged to live long did not have to fight to keep up with the fashions of those who were much younger. Anyhow, that was the only time of the week that Mr. Moseley had a chance to dress up. And dress up he did. But he was not the only one like that.

One of Mr. Moseley's special duties in the church was to count the number of communicants' cards at the start of the service so that he could provide the priest with an accurate count of the number of persons intending to make their communions. Problems often arose when members were very late for the service, after the head-count had already been tallied, or when members insisted in going up to the altar rail for communion without having placed their cards in the designated box at the start of the service. Quite naturally, this annoyed Mr. Moseley no end; and he often had to make an "executive decision" (as he called it), whether to "squeeze them in" the count, or scold them for being so negligent. It all depended on who was the transgressor, for he was well aware of certain members who were habitual violators of the rule. Accordingly, members knew that it was always in their best interest to keep on the good side of Mr. Moseley, even to the point of extending lavish compliments to him for his regular sartorial elegance.

Many of the people in the church made it a habit of showing off what they had just received from America or England. Their relatives in Boston, and Brooklyn, and Miami, and St. Thomas, and Leicester, often sent them these large barrels of clothing. When they unpacked the barrels, the clothing would carry a sweet fragrance, packed as they were among several grocery items. There would be bath soap, perfumes, exercise books and pencils, Uncle Ben's rice, Quaker Oats, Carnation Milk, and Fruit-of-the-loom underwear. Sometimes you could not tell whether the clothes were new, used, old, or very old. You knew that they had a nice sweet smell, and that they had come from America, or England, and occasionally from Toronto. If they had come from America, it was more than likely that nobody else in the church would be dressed in a similar style, or color, that Sunday. Every piece of new clothes had to be worn to church first. If you did not do that, the clothes would not last long, they thought. God would be vexed with you for not wearing it to church first to give thanks for having clothed your nakedness with a blessing from overseas.

But some of the clothes were sometimes unsuited for the climate, or for the bodies on which they were placed. The shoes sometimes created blisters on their toes long before they could reach back home from church. So, it was not unusual to see more than half of the congregation, especially the women, with their shoes off in church massaging their feet during the service except, of course, when they went up for communion limping in pious agony. Sometimes when you heard them singing loudly, it was not because they knew the hymns that well; it was rather because the shoes were burning their feet, and they had to cry out in joyful pain! It was not uncommon to see one person in a new dress this Sunday and to see her sister in the same dress a few Sundays later.

Why was that? It was simply because the first wearer had been forced to concede that she did not look all that nice in the dress from away. So, instead of taking it to the needle-worker for alteration, it was better to pass it on to somebody else for the time being. Whenever that person received another barrel or parcel from America, there would surely be something in there to make good on the exchange. Whether you called used clothes "waggees", or "gi-tuh-muhs", or "han'me-downs", it really did not matter. If they came from America in the parcel, or the barrel, it was worth wearing to church first. The clothes had such a sweet smell that nobody would dare think of them as used clothes. The ladies dressed up in the shoes, the stockings, the hats, the handbags and the wigs, and the gentlemen would show off their cuff-link shirts, their three-piece suits, and their bowties. That was how Mr. Moseley came to be so conspicuous last week. She remembered the bowtie and the awkward way it looked around his neck. Yet, what Moseley lacked in deportment, he certainly made up for it with decency, decorum, and church discipline. She still had great admiration for Mr. Moseley and Teacher Joe. They were indeed devout men of God. But church attire amongst the older folk could often be a cause for constant distraction during the services.

It was not that she was very critical of what people wore. Her mother had often quoted to her a verse from the Bible that spoke about rending one's heart but not one's clothing. She knew all along that the clothes were not all that important, but still she expected people to dress properly. After all they were coming into the Lord's own house, on the Lord's own day, to worship with the Lord's own people, in the Lord's own way. In any event you were expected to put on your Sunday best, and to dress well in coming to church. She had learned in school that long ago the slaves dressed up on Sundays to go to market.

Sunday was no longer market day, for slavery was virtually over now. At least, that is what she was taught. But by the way some of those White people on the Island often behaved, they did not seem to have heard it or believed it. Everybody had heard the news that *Massa day don'!* Some of those people who used to work their souls out for these White people still behaved as if the slave days and the slave ways were alive and well. Not for her though. Slavery was done, done, done! Praise be to the Lord! Market day was now on Saturday, but people should still be dressed as elegantly as possible when they came before the Lord on a Sunday.

III

So, the place where she sat in church here in America was important to her because it reminded her of church at home when she was growing up. That was one of the main reasons why she wanted to be early, just in order to get a good seat. But luck was not on her side. Try as she might, these two little children kept her back and made her late. And that should not be. Her husband was not much of a help with them, because he was half-a-sleep, having come in at four o'clock in the morning from his little extra week-end job. He worked hard during the week at his two jobs. His main job was in construction, for the pay was good, and the benefits were reasonably satisfactory. He and his family were covered by insurance and other medical provisions. But he could never understand why this man they called "Uncle Sam" had to dip his hand so heavily into his pay packet every other week. By the time he brought home something from his main paycheck, he virtually had to go out again to look for more work, to make some extra money.

He had often wondered who this Uncle Sam really was, and how he got his name, and why they thought he was really an uncle. But nobody could put him straight on the matter. All he knew was that Uncle Sam was no uncle to him; for all his uncles used to give him something, but this uncle was always taking something from him. Anyhow, he was not complaining too much, for the little he got here was still much more than what he was used to making back home. So, although he would grumble loudly about the taxes and other deductions, he would quietly say to himself 'God bless Uncle Sam'.

Before he came to America, he used to hear his own Uncle Jack saying so, and he always had a deep respect for anything Uncle Jack said. It was Uncle Jack who had sponsored him in coming to America; but he knew that Uncle Jack could not have brought him without the blessing of Uncle Sam. Even if Uncle Sam was very heavy-handed in what he took out of his pay packet, he still had to be somewhat thankful for these mercies, though smaller than he would really have preferred. He had a job. But he still needed the extra job.

He had this extra job on the weekends, in order to earn the extra cash to send back home to the Islands to look after his other children there. In addition, he was looking forward to the day when he would not have to work so hard in this cold country. It was cold in so many ways. Yet, cold or not, he was saving up as much as he could to pay off for the plot of land in the new estate development, not far from where he was born back home. He had plans to build himself a nice house long before he had to retire finally. He could then go back home for vacations and not have to stay in those expensive hotels with those strange tourists.

That was why he worked so hard seven days a week, fifty weeks a year. He did not mind it if people criticized him for working so hard, and being so thrifty, saving as much money as he could. He was not into buying foolish gadgets and flashy suits, or expensive status symbols. He knew what he had to do, for God gave him the strength and the will to accomplish much. He was determined to work hard to help himself, and his family here, his family back home, and his future. For, after all, America was not home, but it was the place of opportunities, and those were opportunities that his Island home could not afford at this time.

All that work made him awfully tired, and he did not have the mind or energy to get in much church attendance. He felt satisfied that his beloved wife was very religious, very diligent in her allegiance to the Church ("Episcopal", or whatever they called it here). He was more than anxious that their two little ones, aged seven (boy) and five (girl), should be brought up in the fear and knowledge of the Lord. He had been regular at church back home.

As a matter of fact, he had been a server (acolyte) under the tutelage old Canon McConney. In his day, nobody could swing the incense better than he, nor could they send the smoke where it should go as accurately as he could. He was the master thurifer. There was even a time when servers would come from some of the neighboring churches just to watch him do his thing and swing that thing. They wanted to copy the styles that he had perfected in the art of thurifership. Occasionally, he would serve as MC (Master of Ceremonies), but he did not like that too much, because it was too confining.

As the MC, he had to stay inside the sanctuary all the time, and be very prominent, making sure that the other servers did what they were supposed to do. He would have to ensure that the altar-book, called the "Missal", was at the right pages at the right time in the service. He had to make sure that the celebrant had everything he needed to lead the service smoothly. He had to ensure that the candles stayed lit in the face of the strong cross-breezes coming through the open windows. But, as the thurifer, he could spend some of the time outside, keeping the coal fire bright and glowing in the incense-pot, called a "thurible", as well as watching whatever was happening in the church yard. All of that was different here in America. The acolytes here did not seem to know very much about what they were supposed to be doing around the altar. Furthermore, as far as he was concerned, neither did the celebrant seem to have much familiarity with *Ritual Notes*. That was the venerated book that established all the rules for the rites and ceremonies in the Anglican Church world-wide.

These people in the church here could not walk in the shoes of the priests back home, he used to think, especially when it came to the rites and ceremonies of the Mass. He could recall the many times when there were special services such as ordinations, patronal festivals, the bishop's visitations, or even the joint festivals of partner churches. There would be a real High Mass then, and if the bishop was there, he would be the thurifer at the Pontifical High Mass. It was on those special occasions that Ritual Notes, (a religious equivalent to Robert's Rules of Order for parliamentary procedure), was carefully consulted, discussed, interpreted, and implemented. Although the book was written in England, with the Church of England people primarily in mind, not even those English people could follow the rituals as skillfully as those servers back home. They really took their liturgical procedures seriously, for it was a very good way of instilling discipline, deportment, and self-esteem in the minds and lives of those servers back home. If you could serve well at the altar, he used to say, you could go places where non-servers would fear to tread.

Beyond that, it was important for him in those days that things should be done decently and in order in the sanctuary. He regarded the rites and ceremonies as important aids to the sanctity of worship and as means of upliftment for the entire congregation. That was what Canon McConney used to tell him, and he believed it with all his heart. But, this American Anglican style was different, and on the few occasions when he went to church here, it annoyed him to see the sloppy and callous way in which the servers (they called everybody 'acolytes' here) carried out their duties. He just could not stand it. It was not anything like what he was used to at home.

The sermons were not always very arresting, they did not make him feel guilty enough about life; for the preachers seemed very cautious in telling the people the truth as it should be told. Perhaps they were afraid of losing members, or losing pledges, or even losing their jobs, by speaking out. Church here was just not the same; but he was still glad that his wife went. After all, he had read somewhere in the Bible that the church-attending wife's good connections with God made up for the flaws of the non-church-attending husband. So, he could work hard and give the church a rest for a long while. He still sent a donation now and again, and he insisted that his wife gave a good offering (he called it collection) every Sunday. That's why he did not feel too badly about the whole thing. It was good that the children could get something of the religious training he got when he was growing up in the Islands, even if this was very different from what he had known.

She had to dress the children all by herself, and make sure that they looked spic' and span, clean and tidy, neat and shiny, for she knew that all those nosy people in the church would be looking to see what they looked like this morning. It was just like back home. People had not changed at all. But she did not mind that very much for, as nosy as they were, they were also very kind to her in many ways, and they helped her to care for the children whenever she needed a break, or had to make a special run somewhere. Church was family to her, and every Sunday was like a little homecoming. She was prepared to take the whole package of caring relationships in the church. They really meant well, even if they could rub her the wrong way sometimes. But she still wanted to be early this morning.

The little girl had kept her back by not keeping still while she was trying to comb her hair in some special plaits, since the hair was so long. The bows she tied on did not match the dress in the way she wanted them to, so she had to scramble through the drawer to find another set of bows. She now had to plug in the iron to press them out, and then hold down the little girl's head as she tied them tight. Then she would powder her little face to help with the often-uncomfortable temperature in the church. The little boy did most of his dressing for himself, for he was already behaving like a big man. He looked fine to her. She only discovered that he was wearing unmatched socks when she sat him down on the seat in church, while she tried to get him to keep his shoes from knocking against the pew in front. By the time she was finished dressing them, she was tired already; and she knew that she would have to wait quite a few minutes for the bus.

Buses did not run as frequently on Sundays as they did during the week. It really was a sacrifice of time, energy, devotion, and maternal skill to go to church any Sunday morning with two little children and no car. But she went anyhow, because God had been good to her all the time, she would say to herself, and she knew that with such sacrifices as hers God would always be well pleased. So, she always tried to go to church every Sunday, even if she was late occasionally. Better late than never, her mother always said. She certainly knew what that meant with two children to bring up in the right way, church-going and all.

IV

The Collect had just ended, and she joined in a loud Amen with the rest of the congregation while taking her seat to rest her weary bones for a little while on the half-soft, half-soiled cushions. Bad as they were, she thought, they were still better than back home where she sat on those hard benches that they called pews. As a little girl she could not understand why the Pentecostal churches had "benches", but the Anglican churches only had "pews". Both were hard alike; and as far as she was concerned, they were all furniture to aid in worshipping the same God. But here she was ready to listen to the reading of the Word, and, thank God, not by the same reader who did such a bad job at reading last Sunday she was in church. Although it seemed as if she was being critical of the reader, she really did not mean to be.

The reading of the lessons in church meant a lot to her. She remembered when people would do anything to read the lessons in church; for it was a privilege and an honor to be so designated. But it wasn't an easy thing, especially when you had to encounter all those strange names, and Old English words, and funny phrases. She could never forget one reader back home calling "Og the King of Bashan" as "O-Gee King of Bashan"! On another occasion that same reader was reading a lesson from the Book of Ezra, where there was a long list of all the musical instruments mentioned twice in the same lesson. So, having taken the trouble to read out the whole list of instruments the first time, he simply skipped the ordeal the second time by referring to "the above-mentioned orchestra"!

You had to prepare the lesson well, to get the right intonations. You had to have a sense of the correct meaning of the text and take your time in reading. After all, the people listened very attentively, since they did not have the texts to follow for themselves. This was what it called for in her childhood days. She remembered the days when one of her Sunday School teachers, Miss Bryson, who was also a day-school teacher, would be called upon to read the lesson on short notice. It was always a joy and a marvel to see how Miss Bryson would stride to the lectern very elegantly, stand erect with her head held up high so that her voice would be pitched to the back of the church. Then she would take her time in reading the lesson as confidently and as intelligently as if she had been given a week's notice. She always wished that she could do that; and she always judged other readers by that same standard.

That was why the lay reader the last Sunday she was at church was such a disappointment, for he knew he was scheduled to read that day. But he read the lesson as if he was learning the English language for the first time. Thank God, the reader this morning was much better. It was a woman, not a teacher; but her diction was good, the words were carefully pronounced, the sense of what she read was clear. Her speed was measured by an articulation which suggested that she probably had intentions of becoming a priest herself. Somehow, she thought, the women lay-readers seemed to take the lessons more seriously than the men. The men often read as if they were just having a casual conversation, not as if they were reading something very special, something sacred, something very important to themselves and the congregation.

She often wondered why the Rector did not speak to them to get them to read better. Some people said that the Rector was afraid to correct them, because the lay readers were very sensitive and he did not want to offend them, even if they needed correction. After all, there were not that many in the church. Some others said that the Rector had his own theology about bad reading. It was not the actual reading that mattered, he was reported to have said, but the spirit behind the reading, for God would always overlook the mistakes. Some people had heard of this strange theological position on the part of the priest, and they had felt offended by it, since it was an insult to their own intelligence, as well as an affront to their dignity. But they did not deal with it since it was not all that weighty a matter.

They would save their fire for the time when weightier matters came along. And come they would, for this congregation was always moving from one little crisis to another. But the Rector himself was a very nice man, and the people loved him. He took good care of them, especially in times of personal crisis and pastoral challenges. He was often lauded for being very compassionate, always willing to make himself available for families in distress, or children caught upon a mess. So, they would always overlook these little liturgical infelicities on his part. The reading was not a problem today, and the lessons were short. The reading of the psalm was a different matter.

Everybody in the islands knew that the Psalter was really the second Anglican hymnbook, second only to the venerated *Hymns Ancient & Modern*. No other denomination knew how to chant those psalms, or vary those chants, and put feeling into those ancient words as well as the Anglicans did in the Islands. Most of the people who could not read well still knew most of the psalms by heart. They could often be heard humming the tunes and breaking out with the words on the buses, in the cane fields, down by the river where they sometimes washed their clothes when the water was turned off, as it often was. The psalms encompassed much of their spirituality, expressed so well what the hymns could not, and often placed them in a mode of prayer and praise at the same time. They had a special psalm for almost everything, and they often flavored their private prayers with a few verses at a time.

Why was this so? The answer was that Matins and Evensong were regular parts of their Sunday worship diet. The choirs would spend hours and hours rehearsing the psalms during the week; so that when Sunday came, they could lead the congregation with the right pointing and pronunciation. The people always sang the psalms lustily, or heartily, if you preferred that term. The singing was very good back in those days, and they raised the roof with their praises ascending to God. The reading of the psalm here in America was a different story; and it was always a sore spot for her. The choir did not chant the gradual psalm, the organist refused to practice them, for he said that Christians were to *read* the psalms, but the Jews (in liturgical Judaism) were to *chant* them, since they were really a part of the Hebrew Bible.

She had never heard such foolishness in all her life, she had once said to herself. She later discovered that the organist was really covering up because his musical skills were severely limited. He was shielding his limited musicology with a veneer of quaint theology about the sacred scriptures. But she was not buying that. He just could not play the organ well enough to handle the psalms properly. So, this congregation had to resort to reading the psalm every Sunday, and someone was chosen (it looked to her like they were chosen at random) to read the psalm. The reader of the psalm this morning was a lady from West Africa. That was one of the beautiful things about this congregation. It was made up of all sorts of people, all shades and sounds of Afro-Anglicanism, all styles of Afro-culture coming together in a rich tapestry of human diversity, quite reaffirming in its spirit, and mutually enriching in its effect.

That word "diversity" meant so much to her, especially since she had come to America and joined this church. But she had noticed in recent times that it was being used a lot by White people in their churches and places of employment. She remembered those early days when she first came to America how she tried to attend the Episcopal Church that was closest to where she was staying at the time. She had gone there for a few Sundays, but nobody ever welcomed her, or gave her a smile, or made her feel that she was just as much Anglican as they were. The sign outside the church had read *"THE EPISCOPAL CHURCH WELCOMES YOU"*. But she very quickly found out that even they said that they "welcomed you", they would often not speak to you. How could they welcome people without speaking to them?

She soon got the message and tried to find another church where they did not appear to be that prejudiced against her and her "type". That made her painfully aware in those days that those White Anglicans, who called themselves Episcopalians, did not really understand how God worked. How could they forget that God had made people of different races and colors, and how God saw what He had made, and how God had liked all creatures very much? The Book of Genesis said so. Furthermore, her priest back home had always instilled into them that God was no respecter of persons, and that all were equal before God. But here, she often wondered if she was worshipping the same God that they claimed to be worshipping.

After all, they were reading from the same Bible, using the same Book of Common Prayer, singing the same hymns (even if those people did not sing very much). They paid a choir to do the singing for them. Did they think that Heaven had the same class system that they wanted to practice here in the church? So "diversity" was not a word that they seemed to like, nor a style of living and worshipping that they wished to encourage. That was why they never bothered to welcome her as a stranger into their congregation. She therefore looked for another church. She found one where the people looked just like her; and from the word 'go' they were warm, friendly, welcoming, and extremely helpful in getting her settled into the whys and wherefores of America.

All of a sudden now, those same White Episcopalians were talking a lot about "diversity" as if it were a new word which had just come down from heaven. Black people, and homosexuals, and disabled people, and poor people, and immigrants of all kinds, had been around for a long, long time. When they had a chance to practice it, they bluntly refused. Now they were trying to catch up in their own way. She felt deep down that it was only because many of their children had now grown up, and some had come out of the closet about their sexual preferences, and they did not want their children excluded from the churches on those grounds. So, they started talking about "diversity, diversity, diversity" as if a new discovery had just come from Columbus' offspring.

Anyhow, diversity for her in this church was different from diversity for those people who had failed to welcome her into their fellowship. She preferred her kind of diversity more than theirs, even though she knew that, in the final analysis, there was only one Hell and one Heaven. She still loved them anyway, for God had made them just as God had made her. She knew that she could not be a Christian, trying to worship God in Spirit and in truth, if she ever attempted to treat them in the same way that they had treated her when she first came to America. But she loved her church too, and her people; and she often spoke of them as *her people.*

As she sat down to take part in the reading of the psalm then, she treasured the fact of the diversity in this congregation here present, for the psalm was being led by a woman from West Africa. The woman's accent was different from hers, but hers was different from the Rector's, who was an African-American from North Carolina. Her accent was also different from the lay reader who read so badly last week. He himself had come to this country a long time ago and had grown up in Boston before coming to Brooklyn, New York, where he now lived. Brooklyn was a microcosm of Blacks from all over the world. Blacks had to make their living in Brooklyn, as elsewhere, alongside the Jews. The Jews were very strong economically, politically, socially, and religiously throughout America.

But the West Indians, the people from the Islands, as they were so often called, could hold their own. They often did well, even if several thousands of young people from the Islands did not always make full use of their opportunities here in America. This church was a place where the importance of making use of every opportunity was often stressed. As she looked around the church that morning, she could see many of the people who, like her, were trying to make the most of those opportunities and benefits for the sake of their children. These were people who had come from Africa, the Islands, Panama, Belize, Brazil, all over America, and even from Central America. It was a joy to hear them speak, with their different accents, different intonations, and even different ways of expressing the punctuation.

This lady from West Africa was reading the psalm now, and sometimes her way of punctuation was different from most of the congregation that morning, but they all took part in reading the psalm responsively. It was a long psalm, but the Rector had decided that they would only read the first twelve verses that morning. Whenever she saw that, she knew that he had in mind to spend a long time either in the pulpit, or with the announcements. For that congregation always had a lot of business to deal with, information to share, arrangements to make, and people to acknowledge, on a Sunday morning. It was a real town-meeting, mixed with Eucharist and corporate doxology for God's many blessings. As the reading of the psalm ended, however, she could not help remembering back home, and how the choir would have led them in one of those beautiful chants for the entire psalm, for they never shortened the worship of God in those days.

To do that, she used to think, was to compromise the integrity of the sacred text, and miss some of the original intentions of the psalmist, whoever he was. She was never made to feel that women had composed any of those psalms; and it was only recently that she had learned that King David was not really the author of all the so-called "Psalms of David". The setting for that particular psalm resonated in her mind as the reading ended, and, for a moment, she was transported back to her home church in the Islands. She saw herself sitting in that special pew near to the cross-aisle and listening to the choir leading them joyfully in singing the psalm as she always thought it should be sung. They would all stand for the Gloria at the end. She was told that the Gloria at the end of the psalm was liturgically meant to remind the angels that it was coming from a Christian congregation and not from a congregation of Jews, even if the Psalter was actually the Jewish Hymnbook, just as "*Hymns Ancient & Modern*" was the Christian hymnbook. For them, two hymnbooks were better than one.

But this was America, and the reading had ended, and she caught herself just in time to notice that the person about to read the New Testament lesson was the same lady who had helped her find a job last year, after she had been laid off for nearly four months. In this church, they really looked out for one another. No matter what the crisis was, there was always somebody who would come to your rescue. This lady had come to her rescue last year when she was jobless and running out of unemployment benefits. That made her sit up and pay even closer attention to the reading - for both the reader, and what was being read, were of special meaning for her this morning. She could follow the passage with her eyes closed, for she knew that passage so well. The only trouble was that it was being read in the newer version which she did not particularly like. She grew up on the King James Version, and she really did not care much for these new-fashioned ways of presenting the old-time religion, especially when it came to the Word of God.

As the reader proceeded with the lesson, she followed along in her mind with the King James Version. It sounded so much sweeter to her than what she was hearing. It had a musical ring. It was easy to remember; and easier for her since she had learned that same passage by heart in Sunday School back home: You just could not beat that sort of language. It stayed with her as fresh as when she had first learned it so many years ago. She reminded herself that she would write it out for her two little children to learn when they got a little older.

But right now, they were not old enough to retain it, and in any case, they were just beginning to make a little disturbance in the pew as they sat next to her. This might cause some distraction for the people in the immediate vicinity, and she did not want anybody to think that she did not know how to bring up her children properly, especially when it came to their church manners. The situation called for some immediate corrective action. The little boy was hitting his shoes against the pew in front. That was when she noticed that he was wearing odd socks. The little girl had come down from the pew and was sitting on the kneeler facing the pew, as if to set up her own workbench for her own church agenda. Such a project would call for opening her mother's handbag to see if she had remembered to bring some corn-curls for her to munch on during the service.

The corn-curls were necessary, the little girl thought to herself, since she had not had much of a breakfast before she left home this morning. It was always a good thing to have something to eat in church, since they did not give her some of what they gave the adults and the older children whenever they went up there to the altar-rail. They would always pass her over, even if she put out her hands like everybody else. If the priest was in a good mood, he might put his heavy hand on her forehead and mumble some words that she could never understand. But they never gave her anything to eat or drink from that strange-looking cup. They kept it for themselves and the older folks. So, she wanted her corn-curls now, since the adults would get their own food later at the altar-rail and drink something from a shiny long cup that everybody drank from. It was a good thing that she had her own cup and did not have to bring it to church for anybody else to drink from it. All she wanted now was her corn-curls out of her mother's bag.

The situation at that very moment was becoming quite complicated and almost untenable. The lesson was being read. Corn-curls were in demand. Odd socks had been revealed. Boyish pranks were beginning. Old ladies beside her were starting to frown. She had to make a difficult decision about how to keep two restive children in check without giving them a slap to keep them quiet. The New Testament called on them to think carefully about excellence and truth; but she had to shift from that thought to these immediate concerns of family discipline in the public space. Added to all of this, she had her own image and reputation to protect, as well as to project.

She did not want to lose face among these nice people all because of the two children whom God had been pleased to grant to her and her husband. For crying babies and unruly children in church were often seen by some nosy people as a sign of ineffective parenting. Not that she agreed with that idea; but she knew it was there, and, for better or for worse, she had to live with it and work around it some way, somehow. She had always held to the belief, and very strongly too, that crying babies were a distinct asset to any church. They were an assurance that the church had some sort of a future. Further, it was an indication that the church had taken the Scripture seriously to train up a child in the way it should grow. How could anybody train up any child in the way it should grow and not bring that child to church every Sunday? Jesus himself did not have any children, but he once placed somebody's child in his lap and invited all little children to come to him as living little icons of the Kingdom of Heaven.

Some people regarded crying babies as a nuisance. Some people regarded them as a distraction. Some thought of them as spoilt brats in the wrong place at the wrong time. Some even thought of them as signs of what was wrong with the world today, since they really could not remember what they themselves had been like when they were that age. But she was ever so grateful to God for blessing her with the gift of these two beautiful Black children. Black, Black, Black, make no mistake about it. But very, very, beautiful, she thought, no matter how much she abhorred their threatening disturbance here in the house of the Lord, likely to erupt at any minute now.

She loved them with an undying maternal love. They were fully her children. She had labored long and hard to bring them to what they were now. She could remember all that she had gone through to bring them into this world. And she did not care what anybody had to say about them. As far as she was concerned, there were people whom she knew sitting in this very church, who were trying desperately to have a child or two, but with no success. All she had to do at this moment in church was to think. That why she said to herself, "think!"

Section Two

Brother Cleibert's Pilgrimage

I

Cleibert Bynoe was very excited about his trip to America. He had been making plans for it for a very long time and had saved enough money to cover most of his expenses. He confidently expected that when he got to Brooklyn, New York, his cousins would be more than willing to offer him some financial assistance to make up any shortfall, since he had heard how well off, they were up there. After all, things were hard in Barbados. Jobs were scarce. The cost of living was high. The funds at his disposal were severely limited. Saving for this trip had caused him to make far too many sacrifices already; but he had always consoled himself that it would be a very worthwhile visit to America. He was going on a visit to America as an Anglican tourist. He had heard so much about the vast differences in Anglicanism in America, and about the distinctive nature of the Black Church in that country. He wanted to see some of it for himself. As he left Barbados bright and early that morning in May, his first stop would be Miami.

He was flying to Miami via BWIA, a Caribbean airline based in Trinidad, with one of the safest records in aviation history. The captain had informed the passengers that the weather on route was forecast to be fine, and that there was a strong breeze in the area which would help to facilitate an uneventful and comfortable flight. There was a strong possibility, he said, that they would arrive a little ahead of schedule. Cleibert felt good about this; so good that he did not bother to open his little Bible which he had brought along for the ride, just in case he felt the spiritual urge to offer up some special devotions in anticipation of some atmospheric turbulence. He had often sung the psalm about

43

those who went down to the seas in ships and occupied their business in great waters. They had seen the works of the Lord, and his wonders in the deep. But there was no psalm about those who went up to the skies in airplanes. He only knew about the heavens declaring the glory of God, and about the firmament declaring God's handiwork. What that "firmament" was, he was not quite sure. But a little special reading of the Bible during some bumps in the flight would at least help to calm his nerves on this his very first flight in any aircraft.

The flight to Miami was to take about three and a half hours; so Cleibert not only expected to be served a substantial meal on board (not those unattractive snacks served on many American airlines about which he had heard so much). He also expected to be engaged in conversation with some stranger. This he certainly looked forward to, since it would help to relieve some of the boredom of the long flight. Three and a half hours was very long for him, since most Caribbean islands were not far from each other. It would also help to distract his attention from the various noises and movements of the aircraft, about which he had heard much from those who had often made the trip between Barbados and America. Sure enough, Cleibert did not have to wait very long for a lively conversation; for, sitting next to him was a young White man who immediately broke the ice by asking him, "Are you going on a shopping trip to Miami?"

"Not really," replied Cleibert. "I am not a businessman as such, I am actually going on a sort of pilgrimage."

"Pilgrimage!" the man exclaimed, gracefully, quietly, but firmly. "Why would anybody choose America for a pilgrimage? Are there holy places there?"

"You tell me," answered Cleibert. "Aren't you an American? Your accent virtually gives you away."

"Yes, I am. My name is Tony, Tony Brussard, and I am just returning from Barbados where I was doing some missionary work for my church. I am a Mormon. We have been engaged in some very exciting evangelism there among your people. We have already built two lovely churches. I guess you could say that I have been on a pilgrimage to your country. That's why it struck me as ironic that you were making one to mine. What kind of pilgrimage are you on?"

"And my name is Cleibert Bynoe, pleased to meet you! I am an Anglican lay-reader in my church in St. Michael, Barbados, and I am making a journey of a lifetime to your country. I have noticed that your Mormon colleagues have been making great strides in my country, and I have even been amazed at the speed in which your two church buildings went up. Those must have been built with American money, right?"

"Yes, we Mormons are very committed to putting our money where we put our mouths. This gives us an even greater appeal than some of the other overseas-based church organizations which flood the mission fields with pamphlets and old clothes, fine promises and sweet performances, without delivering many tangible and lasting benefits."

"Well, there are missionaries and missionaries," replied Cleibert. "My main problem with all of them is that they visit our little countries in the Caribbean and make us all believe that we are so bad, so much in danger of hell-fire; but they seem to turn their backs on what is happening in their own countries. Why can't they leave us to preach our own Gospel in our own way to our own people? Anyhow, I trust that you had a lovely visit to Barbados. How long did you stay?"

"Three weeks."

"Was that all? What could you accomplish in three weeks?"

"I plant, another waters, and God gives the increase!"

"Yeah, that's biblical enough! I am going to America to check out the increase among Anglicans for myself."

"Are there Anglicans in the States? I've never heard of any."

"Of course, there are! You perhaps know them as Episcopalians, members of the Episcopal Church. Well, they are the same church-people. Episcopalians are American Anglicans. But I understand that there have been so many little splinter groups among them these days that several of them have chosen different titles for their organizations, all of them claiming to be the true Anglicans. It is still true to say, however, that all Episcopalians are Anglicans, but all Anglicans are not Episcopalians. A few weeks ago, an American lady attended a service at our church. She was a White tourist staying at a nearby hotel. After the service she told my priest that she enjoyed the service very much, especially as it was the first time in her life that she had ever attended an Anglican service. When my minister asked her what church she attended back home, she said that she was an Episcopalian!"

"That's interesting. We Mormons do not suffer from many wide divisions, even though there are some splinter factions here and there. But, tell me; why would you, a Black Barbadian, be so interested in making a pilgrimage to visit Episcopalians in America? All the Episcopalians I know are White."

"I find your question interesting too, because I thought that all Mormons were supposed to be White. But you and your colleagues have been making Mormons out of our Black people in Barbados. A Black Mormon is an oddity to me, and certainly a much stranger character than a Black Episcopalian. The Anglican Church in Barbados is a Black church, even if it was started by White men over three hundred years ago. I have been an Anglican all my life, and all my relatives, parents, grand-parents, and great-grand-parents have all been Anglicans. Anglicanism for me has always been a Black experience. As a matter of fact, I understand that the Anglican Communion, which is made up of all the Anglican churches throughout the world, is really a non-White global reality. I was reading somewhere recently where it is claimed that the typical member of the Anglican Church, on a global scale, is a young Black female who is under thirty years of age, and whose native language is not English. But I don't know how true that is. But that should make all White Anglicans sit up and take note that they essentially belong to a church in which they are not in the majority. So, my pilgrimage to America is partly to observe how Black Episcopalians are living out their global majority status in a local minority context. We all belong to the Big Church!"

Just then, the flight attendant reached their row, and interrupted the flow of their conversation by offering them some breakfast. Cleibert half-welcomed the interruption, for he was quite hungry and had eagerly looked forward to this feeding moment on this his historic first flight. But he also half-resented it because he was anxious to see how his fellow-traveler would handle his latest observations. Cleibert was anxious to see what kind of meal BWIA would serve since he had often heard of their exquisite menus, far different from the quality of food served on some other airlines. He happened to choose the flying-fish-and-bakes breakfast, while his neighbor opted for the traditional ham-and-eggs. That choice surprised him somewhat, for he had always believed that the Mormons had as strict a religious diet as the Seventh Day Adventists - avoiding pork and pork products at all costs. Both quietly settled down to their respective meals.

"I was thinking about what you were saying just now," said the American. "I was always under the impression that Blacks were either Baptists, or Methodists, or Pentecostalists. The Episcopalians have had a history of being very elitist, with various episodes of racism in their history. I used to think that Blacks would never want to be a part of such a religious grouping."

"It's very funny that you should say that" said Cleibert. "Because that's exactly the kind of picture I have of your church and its people. The stories I have heard about Mormons have not been favorable to Blacks at all, and yet, you folks have just been boasting about your ten million membership world-wide, Blacks included."

"Ordinarily," said Brussard, "I expect Blacks to have little or nothing to do with institutions which had their hands dirtied with slave-ownership. But now, you tell me that there are Black congregations all over the States. What do you think accounts for this?"

"That's exactly the kind of thing I am going to your country to find out. One thing I know is that the Blacks in the States have never had an easy time with the practice of their religion in the company of Whites. As a matter of fact, I was reading just recently where in the late eighteenth century a man named Richard Allen had been forcibly ejected from the White Methodist church. As a result of that fiasco, not only did the African Methodist Episcopal Church come into being, but his colleague Absalom Jones eventually became the first Black to be ordained a deacon in the Episcopal Church.

"But Jones had a very hard time. I am scheduled to visit the church which he started in Philadelphia, St. Thomas', as a part of my pilgrimage. A straight answer to your question would have to consider the thousands and thousands of people from the West Indies who have migrated to the States over the years. My relatives in Brooklyn, for example, have known no other denomination but the Anglicans. They were born Anglicans, and they will die Anglicans, regardless of the discomforts they sometimes experience in the Episcopal Church."

"That's fine; but what about the Blacks who are not from the Islands. How do you account for their participation and membership in the Episcopal Church?"

Cleibert realized that he was being called upon here to explain something about the demographics of another country where he had never been before. He had to think very quickly about how to deal with this test of his intelligence, this probing of his knowledge. If he claimed not to be able to answer a simple question like this one, he might appear to be less than knowledgeable about the Anglican Communion as a whole, or about Black people. He had often heard of this tendency on the part of non-Blacks to assume that any Black could speak for every Black, or that every Black knew every other Black. He had come across such a situation before where a White couple had very politely inquired whether he knew a certain Black, whom they had met at a wedding, and who looked very much like him. On that occasion he had to explain to his White friends that just as all Whites did not know each other neither did all Blacks.

But, apart from being a Black man, he was also a Black Barbadian. Barbadians were supposed to have an international reputation for being very bright, highly literate, widely read, and very conversant with global affairs. After all, this was not only why Barbados was often called "Little England", but also why the Anglican Church had been so successfully established there. So, he had the reputation of his whole country to defend and protect in the company of this American stranger. He launched into some American history, hoping against hope that his friend would find a satisfactory answer to this awkward question somewhere along the way.

"My dear friend, Mr. Brussard, one of the things which is so often forgotten by Americans is that they are still in the initial stages of a social and political experiment which began some centuries ago when that European sailor, Christopher Columbus, made that colossal navigational mistake and ended up in the wrong place. His mistake became the great misfortune for the original owners of what is now called America. I have never heard what the land was called before it was renamed America. Do you know?"

"No, I'm afraid not," said Brussard. "But I must check that out when I get back."

"The point I am making," Cleibert continued, "is that America as we know it today is essentially a country of immigrants. Apart from the original inhabitants, the Native Americans, as they are unfortunately called, all the other folk there came from elsewhere, Europe, Africa, Asia, the Caribbean, and the Americas. When they came, they brought certain institutions with them. But at an early stage, the people in the New World established some new institutions of their own, because they wanted to express their originality, their freedom and independence, as well as their sense of power. That accounted for the emergence of so many different Christian denominations in your country, as far as I understand. Even your own denomination of Mormonism was an American creation, directly related to some of your people's stories."

"That's quite true," said Brussard, "Mormons found their genesis in my country."

Cleibert continued, "So, when the new immigrants came, they had one of three choices - join the established churches, start their own churches, or stay away from all churches. But, since churches are a form of socio-economic-political activity in a country as new as yours, it always made sense to join some established denomination, at least for the social contact. You call it 'networking' in some quarters. I understand that this accounts for many of the Whites who are Episcopalians today. They were not born Episcopalians, but the Episcopal Church offers them some steady corridors of upward mobility, since many rich and powerful Americans are Episcopalians. I am told that many Whites have joined the Episcopal Church out of self-interest (whether enlightened or not), or because of the liberal image for which it is commonly known.

"But I have also heard that many of them are attracted by the Anglican traditions of worship and order, as well as by the broad strokes which govern the Anglican theological culture and spiritual climate. Of course, we Anglicans are often misunderstood, for outsiders say that we stand for anything, and therefore are good for nothing. But that's unfair! We just recognize that God does exist at the end of anybody's theology, neither is God a theologian, as some fundamentalists would have us believe.

"With the Blacks who join, many of them have come from the West Indies and Africa where they were already Anglicans from birth. As far as the African Americans are concerned, I imagine that some are cradle Episcopalians, some going back for a few generations emerging out of the newly emancipated slave societies. But many have opted to join the Episcopal Church for practically the same reasons that Whites leave their cradle denominations to become Episcopalians. Some of them have said that it is much more economical to be a Black Episcopalian than a Black Baptist, for you get to keep more of your money away from all those multiple collections, and tithes, and special projects. It is partly a power thing, or a matter of religious taste and lifestyle, partly a social mobility thing, and partly a religious preference thing.

"In other words, the Episcopal Church, as far as I have read about it from a distance, is a dynamic microcosm of America itself - it is a community of immigrants from other denominations and countries. It is not as bad as the Church of England, which some people refer to as the British Conservative Party at prayer; but it is not far from being the American social mosaic at work in a religious laboratory. It is a very socially rich and culturally diverse religious community. The Episcopal Church is still evolving, and all sorts of social experiments are still being tested, like Black cathedral deans, women bishops, gay and lesbian rectors, multi-lingual liturgies, or even the blessing of same-sex unions. It is all part of the Big Church"

"Wow!" said Brussard, "That's quite a mouthful! Did you learn about all of this in preparation for your pilgrimage?"

"Some of it, yes; but I have been an avid student of Anglican history for quite some time now. I have taken a few courses at Codrington College, where priests have been trained for the Anglican ministry in the West Indies and Africa since 1830. As a matter of fact, the first Black bishop in the Church of England, Wilfred Wood, was a Barbadian who was trained at Codrington. There are also many other bishops and prominent Anglicans who are graduates of that institution. The first Black bishop of Bermuda, Ewen Ratteray, was also a Codrington graduate."

"I really must commend you for your knowledge of your church, Mr. Bynoe. I can see that you are a staunch member of your denomination and would clearly benefit immensely from this pilgrimage. What cities do you plan to visit in the States, and which churches?"

"Well, it all depends on how expensive it is to get around the country," said Cleibert. "For I really do not have a lot of money, and I understand that travel costs can be quite high. However, if all goes well, I plan to visit a large church in Miami, one in Baltimore, one in Philadelphia, and one in Brooklyn. If I get the chance, I'd also love to visit Washington to see the White House, the Capitol Building, and the Washington National Cathedral, and the Martin Luther King Jr. Memorial. I hear there was a Black Dean at that Cathedral, and that he was not originally an Anglican. I also understand that the first Black Episcopal Bishop of Washington was not originally Anglicans either! But that's a good thing; just as I hear that a Bishop of Utah was once a member of your Church. That speaks to the richness and diversity of the Episcopal Church I was mentioning earlier. It is all part of the Big Church."

Just then, their attention was drawn to some program on the television screen in front of them, and the conversation more or less came to an end. While Brussard eventually settled into a semi-sleeping position, Cleibert turned his attention for the rest of the flight to checking over his travel documents for immigration authorities, scanning the free literature in the seat pocket in front of him, and generally enjoying the smooth flight to Miami on the tip of Florida's south coast.

The flight arrived on time. Cleibert bid farewell to Brussard in the arrival hall, for, as usual, American citizens were treated with a special deference unavailable to visitors and permanent residents to the United States. Brussard wended his way with ease through the lines to the customs hall, while Cleibert inched his way forward through

Immigration and Customs without too much difficulty. When he emerged from the customs hall with his luggage, he could not help remembering some of the horror stories he had heard from previous travelers about the hassle they had experienced with the Customs and Immigration authorities. He was not that unlucky. This provided for him a good omen about the pilgrimage on which he was now fully embarked, having been granted sufficient time to visit the churches, and having assured the authorities that he had every desire and intention to return his native land, God's own country, Barbados, at the end of his visit to America.

II

_____

The sun rose early over the Miami skies on the Sunday morning. Cleibert felt very much at home in this tropical-like part of America. It reminded him so much of the typical Barbadian tropical sunrise, with the beams of morning light spreading their radiance over the blue Caribbean Sea. There were no long coats to be seen anywhere; that assured him of the warmth and breezy climate of which he had been reading on the flight from Barbados. People were dressed as casually as the people in the Islands. The only difference was that it just did not look like Sunday to him, as he knew it in Barbados. Stores were open, but not the office buildings. People were heading to the beaches and parks in great numbers. There was little evidence that church-going was a major social activity in Miami, in spite of the fact that he had already passed by innumerable church buildings - buildings large and small, with varying architectural designs, and different sign-boards, in Spanish, French (or was it Creole (?), Korean (?), and some other languages which to him were intensely foreign.

The taxi in which he was riding was taking him to St. Martha's Episcopal Church. He had originally made the mistake of asking the driver to take him to the St. Martha's Anglican Church at a certain address. The taxi-driver had promptly retorted that he had been living and working in Miami for over 35 years, and so far as he knew there were no Anglican churches in the city.

"Surely, there must be many Anglican churches in such a large city!" Cleibert had exclaimed. "I know many Anglicans who live here, and to the best of my knowledge and belief they have never changed their religion."

"I can't speak about your friends, Sir," replied the driver, "but I can certainly tell you about the churches. We have no Anglican churches in Miami, period! You must have come to the wrong city!"

Just then, Cleibert checked himself, remembering that he was in America, after all, and that many people did not know what was meant by the term "Anglican". He had heard that many of his people who migrated to America were often confused about the absence of Anglican churches, and had not been informed, prior to their departure from home, that the Episcopal Church was the same denomination as the Anglican church in their home country. Many people from the Islands had thus joined some other denomination since they could not find any Anglican churches anywhere. He promised to raise that question with various church officials during his pilgrimage to America. But for the moment he himself had forgotten the distinction.

"Do you know any Episcopal churches then?" Cleibert asked.

"Sure, many of them - big ones, little ones, White ones, black ones, some by the sea, many in the suburbs, none of them Spanish-speaking though."

"Why is that?"

"Because those Episcopal churches strike me as being only interested in English, as if that's the only language which God speaks!"

"You mean that there are no Spanish-speaking Episcopal churches that you know of, in spite of the large Hispanic population in the area?"

"That's right. If there are any, I don't know of them. But it really does not matter to me, anyhow, for I am not interested. I take the folks to any church they wish to attend; make my money, support my kids, send some assistance back home to the old folks, and worship my God in my own way, in my own little church."

"Where is that?"

"The church of St. Mattress-and-the-Holy-Pillow! Home!"

"Do your children also worship there as well?"

"No, they go to a Catholic church, but I prefer to pass up on all that organized religious stuff. I just stick to making an honest living six-and-a-half days a week. My God understands."

By the time they arrived at St. Martha's Church, there was a brisk traffic of Black churchgoers in front of the large edifice, some making their exit and others making their entrance. He looked carefully to see if there were any Whites in the crowd, but none were to be found. He had noticed one of the famous signs outside the church, prominently displayed, as was typical of most Episcopal churches throughout the country. The sign proudly read: *THE EPISCOPAL CHURCH WELCOMES YOU.* He would now begin to get a sense of how true that traditional sign meant what it said. For he had heard it said that there was a clear distinction between White churches and black churches in America, and that there was not that great surge of welcome for all sorts and conditions of people as the sign wanted the public to believe.

Indeed, coming from Barbados, where they had long passed that stage of segregation, he found it strange that such a color distinction was so deeply entrenched in the American ways of life. Was that a sign of social backwardness in this the richest and most powerful country, he wondered. Or was it simply a convenient way of exercising social control through peaceful co-existence and ethnic religious diversity? Someone had told him that 11AM on Sundays in America was the most divisive and segregated hour of the week. But here he was, attending a 10:30AM service. Was that segregated too? Were they worshipping the same God, or what? As much as it had puzzled him, Cleibert was determined not to allow such an apparent blemish on the meaning of Christian solidarity to interfere with his pilgrimage.

After all, he mused, solidarity did not always involve uniformity. As a born and bred Anglican, he had learned that only too well. But he could not help wondering if the American Anglicans had not taken this lack of uniformity too far, for too long, especially in this "the land of the free and home of the brave." If they could be brave about war, why they couldn't be brave about race, he wondered. Nevertheless, he was prepared to keep an open mind, devoid of cynicism or disdain, at least for the duration of his sojourn in America. But it was hard, he said to himself, it was hard.

It was immediately obvious to Cleibert that he was about to enter into a new experience of a large congregation of worshippers, in a church which had to accommodate its members by arranging several Sunday morning services. He had learned beforehand that the two earlier services of the day were not as bright and colorful as the 10:30 AM Choral Eucharist.

He was particularly anxious to witness St. Martha's at its finest, with smells and bells, music and ritual, holy smoke and holy water. He had heard much about its high church propensities and was desirous of getting a feel for the way in which Black Episcopalians interpreted their Anglo-Catholic traditions. After all, Barbados had been famous for its wide variety of church-styles - some high, some low, and some broad - but he was told that he should not expect to find many low-church expressions of Anglicanism during his pilgrimage. St. Martha's was to be his first experience of vintage Black high-church religion. And what an experience it was to be!

He was warmly welcomed by a male usher who was dressed in a special uniform - a tan blazer with a crest on the breast pocket displaying some religious symbol, a clearly marked lapel-pin on which the word "Usher" was duly inscribed. The attire was elegantly matched with a pair of cream trousers, a pastel-colored necktie with a Windsor knot, and a pair of white gloves which showed signs of being wearied and worn from frequent manual greetings. There was a team of four ushers, similarly dressed, all performing the same functions of greeting the worshippers, handing them the church leaflets and other pieces of literature, and intimating suitable places for them to be seated.

Cleibert introduced himself as a visiting Anglican from Barbados and was promptly ushered to a seat in the nave some nine or ten pews away from the high altar. It was the Sunday after the Ascension, so the floral arrangements, the paraments in the sanctuary, the Eucharistic vessels already set out on the altar, the six candlesticks in front of the reredos, and the red cushions at the base of the communion rails all made Cleibert feel very much at home. The hymn numbers on the board did not ring a bell, for he was accustomed to a different hymnal at home in Barbados. He had grown up on *Hymns Ancient & Modern* and knew most of the seven hundred and seventy-nine hymns in that book by their numbers. As far as he was concerned that was the only hymnbook which angels and archangels used in heaven. He was confirmed in this opinion especially as the very last hymn in that book began with the words: "There was joy in Heaven". But he was not inclined to press his point this early in his American pilgrimage, for, after all, some room had to be made for a wider repertoire within the pearly gates above.

The service did not begin promptly as scheduled, and this gave Cleibert a little more time to get a better view of his fellow-congregants, without turning around to conspicuously to give himself away as a stranger in church. He took careful note of the leaflet he had received. He found himself being particularly amazed at the wide variety of notices, announcements, advertisements, reminders. There was a plethora of organizational information, and official pronouncements, prayer-lists and personal notes, financial statements and subtle warnings, which were all being communicated to the Lord's own people, in the Lord's own house, on the Lord's own day. This was nothing like the simple leaflet which his church in Barbados usually issued on Sundays. Many of those notices and advertisements would be rather found in the secular newspapers during the week, not in the church bulletin.

It did not take Cleibert very long to opine that a Black church gathering such as this was much more than a religious event, if the church leaflet he was perusing was anything to go by. It had the makings of a town meeting, a fellowship hall, a mutual exchange society, a forum for organizational interactions and personal healing, an informal program of general education for social and political awareness, as well as a gathering of folk known to each other over the years, who wished to catch up with the latest happenings and get a fresh impetus to face the world during the coming week. That leaflet itself was so loaded with social concerns and pastoral leads, that Cleibert Bynoe almost immediately began to rethink his own incipient theology about the word "church". When it came to be associated with Blacks, he said to himself, the word "Church" had all the makings of a verb and far less those of a noun. These people had come here to St. Martha's to **do** church, not just to **be in** church. But they all belonged to Big Church.

Although there was something un-Anglican about it, he thought, it still represented who these people were as gathered in God's name. So, if God did not mind it, why should he? More and more people were coming to the recognition that God was not an Anglican. God was not even a Christian, someone had once said to him. That statement has shocked him at first. But with every new expression of religious symbol and activity, such as he was now about to witness here in Miami, and presumably done with the utmost sincerity and noblest of meaning, Cleibert Bynoe, the Anglican lay-reader from Barbados, who thought that he had such a firm grasp of the Anglican ethos and its ecclesial traditions, was already beginning to experience a slight trickle of personal liberation from his own Anglican fixations. If it was true that the Episcopal Church was still evolving, it was also true that he himself, as a lifelong Anglican, was still evolving too. It was generally an Anglican thing. It certainly made him even more keenly aware of the wider meaning of belonging to the Big Church, the Anglican Communion.

Apart from the unusual choir-robes, the participation of the laity in the readings of lessons and prayers, the inclusion of some Gospel songs at the time of communion, there was nothing in the liturgy at St. Martha's which was particularly strange to Cleibert. He felt very much at home with the liturgy, for it had all the marks of the standard Anglican Eucharist, patterned, thank God, on the Book of Common Prayer. The Scripture readings were taken from the *New Revised Standard Version*, and the text of the psalm was somewhat unfamiliar. Nevertheless, he found himself making the translations in his own mind from the modern to the "King James Version" with which he had been so familiar, and the psalm from the good old Cranmerian version of the Psalter. The psalm was read, and not chanted. This was a slight disappointment to him; having become so accustomed to the liturgical principle that the psalms were originally written for liturgical chanting rather than solemn recitation.

Cleibert felt very at home, despite these few differences. The large congregation sang with great gusto; and this surprised Cleibert somewhat, for he had heard that Episcopalian congregations relied very much on their choirs to do most of the singing. This did not appear to him to be the case in this service. These people sounded more like Caribbean folk! He was soon to discover that he was mainly right. During the exchange of the peace, one of the persons in the pew in front of him turned around to share the greeting, and quickly noted that Cleibert had a strong Barbadian accent. Barbadians have great difficulty in disguising their accents, Cleibert soon realized. The lady readily acknowledged that she herself was from the Bahamas, from Abaco actually, and that most of the members of St. Martha's were of Bahamian origin or extract. This explained why there were so many references to programs related to Bahamians in Miami and the Diocese of Nassau and the Bahamas. It also explained why there was a fund-raising drive for the support of one of the Anglican churches in the Bahamas which had been damaged in a recent hurricane.

The Coffee Hour which followed the service was remarkable for the absence of coffee. The refreshments consisted of drinks made from local fruit, cakes and patties, conch fritters, chicken wings, meatballs, and johnny-cakes. Johnnycakes were a Bahamian specialty which characterized most festive occasions at St. Martha's. This part of the church fellowship was unusual for Cleibert, since there were rarely any such refreshments served after services at his church in Barbados. People just chatted casually with each other in the church yard or wended their way to the nearest bus-stop for the ride back home. It was at this point that Cleibert had the chance to speak with the Rector, Canon Burton, who had presided at the Eucharist upstairs and preached the sermon. The usher who had greeted Cleibert at the front door had made sure that the Rector made time to speak with him now.

"Welcome to St. Martha's," began Canon Burton, "is this your first visit to Miami?"

"Yes, it is," said Cleibert. "Actually, this is my very first time outside of Barbados!"

"My usher tells me that you are visiting the States as part of an Anglican pilgrimage. What does that entail?"

"Well, you see, Canon, I have been an Anglican all my life. I have grown up knowing the Anglican Church in certain sort of way. I was regular in Sunday School. I sang in the choir as a boy. I was a server for many years, until they promoted me to be a Lay reader. Right now, I am a licensed chalicist, having done several special courses in religious studies at Codrington College. My purpose on this trip is to see how another sector of the Anglican Church lives, especially other Blacks. As you know, I come from a part of the world where Blacks are in the majority. So, I am very interested in observing how Black Anglicans make out in a predominantly White church, given all the history of racism and prejudice about which I have read so much. Is there anything you would like to share with me along these lines?"

"There certainly is," answered Burton, "but I am afraid I have to deal with some other matters fairly urgently. As you can see, we have quite a large congregation here, and most of these members are only available for church business on Sunday mornings since they are working so hard during the week. Many of them at two, and sometimes three jobs. So, I need to catch them when I can, and they know how to get at me in a rush on Sundays. Let's try and meet on Tuesday morning, will you still be here?"

"Yes, I leave on Wednesday for Baltimore," said Cleibert. "But one quick question, Canon. That name of yours, Burton, is a Barbadian name. Do you have any Bajan connections?"

"I wondered when you would ask that!" replied the priest. "My father came from Barbados over fifty years ago, settled in Florida, and married a Bahamian. So I am part Bajan and part Bahamian. I have never acquired the Barbadian accent, but I understand it very well, having grown up with it at home. Please give me a call on Tuesday morning, and we'll get together."

Cleibert Bynoe felt very encouraged by his brief encounter with Canon Burton. It virtually gave him the kind of passport he was looking for to make his way through the small huddles of congregants conversing among themselves in the Fellowship Hall. He was able to meet a wide cross-section of the congregation by the time it was over. He learned much about the struggles in the church to meet the annual budget, to secure the services of sufficient teachers for the Sunday School, to get the members to turn in the "ticket-money" from the recent jumble-sale, and to get the youths of the church to keep their playing area of the church-hall in a much tidier condition. All these problems and concerns seemed all too familiar to him. It sounded very much like home, to such an extent that he began to wonder if there were common "diseases" from which most Anglicans suffered, regardless of their social context or their ethnic background. He would have to check into this much further, as the pilgrimage progressed, he thought to himself.

The atmosphere in the Hall was warm and friendly. Several persons welcomed him, compared notes with him about their respective churches, shared their experiences from tourist-cruises they had made down the Islands, being very careful, of course, to single out Barbados for special praise. He was particularly struck by the styles of dresses and suits they wore and noted the striking similarity between standards of dress for church between Barbados and St. Martha's. Since he had not visited any other church so far, he could only restrict his opinion to the people here at this church.

They dressed well, he thought, and this suggested to him that there was a special reverence for the house of the Lord, not unlike the spirituality of attire under which he had grown up in Barbados. You never went to church dressed in any casual or inappropriate way. It was out of reverence for God that people were to wear their Sunday-best. There were church-clothes, work-clothes, sports-clothes, and home-clothes in the closet, and God always deserved the best.

The people at St. Martha's obviously shared a similar set of values. It made a statement all its own, he thought, about how seriously they took their participation in the Sunday morning worship and fellowship experience. Even if it might be granted that there was a suspicious element of ostentation, a showing-off, a "fashion-show" atmosphere in some quarters at home in Barbados, this did not readily appear to be the case here. The people looked nice and comfortable, and since all were well dressed, there would be no conspicuous models to applaud.

God deserved the best attire they had, and here they were, offering it all to each other and God, on this the Lord's day, in the Lord's house.

Cleibert caught a taxi and made his way back to his friend's house some twenty minutes away from St. Martha's. There he was able to catch up on what happens on a Sunday afternoon and evening in Miami, all quite different from the Barbadian way of life on a Sunday. For one thing, Evensong was out of the question here; for it was clear to him that God's business closed early on Sunday's in order to allow for other forms of entertainment and recreation on Sundays, even for those who had been to church in the morning. As he tried to enjoy the hospitality of his host, however, Cleibert could not help reflecting very intensely on two troubling questions.

One, how did a Sunday morning at St. Martha's tie in with a Sunday evening in Miami? Two, what would carry these people through the week and bring them back to St. Martha's next Sunday morning? In other words, what role did the Black Anglican expression of the Christian faith play in liberating, enhancing, and sustaining the lives and hopes of the people with whom he had just worshipped? As far as he was concerned, he thought to himself, Sunday morning was either a fly in these people's ointment, or else it was a balm in the Gilead of their experiences and expectations. He would raise these issues with Canon Burton on Tuesday morning.

III
___

The two hours of conversation between Canon Burton and Cleibert Bynoe were frequently interrupted by telephone calls and knocks on the office door. Burton had to apologize quite profusely for these, explaining that there was no other way of dealing with these demands on his time from so many of his parishioners. St. Martha's, Burton explained, was a hive of activity throughout the whole week, since for many of the parishioners the church was perhaps their only home away from home. Furthermore, many members who had problems with civic authorities, or crises of one kind or another, could not afford the professional services in the community, and therefore had to rely on the assistance of the church. This meant, of course, that the Rector of the parish found himself wearing many, many, hats during any one weekday.

Additionally, although this was an Episcopal church, it was still an integral part of the Black Church in America. For most Blacks in this country, Burton suggested, the Black Church was the only solid and stable institution which Black people had, and which they could truly call their own. They therefore had to rely very heavily on the services of the Black Church, whether Episcopal, Methodist, Baptist, Pentecostal, Church of God, or otherwise, to function on their behalf as advocate, advisor, social welfare agency, hospital, social educator, recreational center, or moral guide, just to name a few. Because there were so few financial resources available to our people, and because they had to stretch those resources so far among themselves and their own people here and overseas, they could not support a very large church budget, and the staffing of our Black churches generally, for week-day operations, was almost universally severely restricted. Therefore, Burton had to wear so many hats, with only the assistance of a part-time priest whose secular occupation prevented him from being of much help during the week.

"Was this also true of White churches?" asked Cleibert.

"In some instances, yes, but not generally so in this part of the country."

"Do you mean that the White churches have much more money and staffing at their disposal?"

"You sure got that right," replied Burton, "and there is very little effort made on their part to offer much assistance and sharing of resources with their Black counterparts. Partnership in the Episcopal Church is almost a bad word for most parishes, except when there is likely to be a patronizing arrangement between a very rich parish in this country and a very poor parish in Latin America or Africa, for example. Charity and sharing never seem to begin close to home. So, Black churches must struggle for their survival almost entirely on their own. But we have never viewed that as the worst thing that could happen to us, for it is better to be poor and free than less poor and uncomfortable. For, in this country, my Dear Sir, everything carries a price. So, our poor Black churches with scarce resources, limited staff, incessant demands, frequent crises, and limited facilities, are still our little castles of freedom and social belonging. These are places of holy ground for us, and we make the most of the little we have without excuse or explanation."

"This certainly helps to answer a question I was posing to myself since Sunday," said Bynoe, "for I was wondering how much the Sunday morning activity here was related to what happened in these people's lives for the rest of the week. I was struck by the fact that in your sermon on Sunday you dwelt on the problems of immigration and the new welfare laws. I was curious to know if these were matters for the priest to deal with in the pulpit rather than for the lawyers and the politicians in the wider society. You seem to have some very strong feelings about the recent changes in social legislation now sweeping the country."

"You see, my dear brother", said Burton, "if the Black Church does not speak *to* the people, *for* the people, and *with* the people, about the things that are itching them, and itching them very severely, I might add, who else do you think will scratch for them? Who else do you think will take up their cause and come to their defense, in some cases, and to their rescue in other cases? What you must understand is that America is being rapidly swept away not only by an increasing incidence of greed in places of power and authority, but also by a tidal wave of xenophobia and ethnocentrism. This country of immigrants has turned on its immigrants, and many of my members who you saw sitting in those pews last Sunday are feeling increasingly unwelcome here, although they have given so much of their blood, sweat, and tears just to survive.

"So, I have no alternative but to speak out, and to offer them the best advice, the noblest ideals, the strongest words of assurance and hope which my theological reflection and moral authority have to offer. This is a fight, brother, a real fight, not only against flesh and blood, but against principalities and powers on the streets, in uniforms, in shops and corporate offices, in board rooms and laboratories, even in church conventions and shopping malls. America is suffering from hospitality fatigue, and the church seems to be catching the symptoms very steadily, if it has not already broken out with the disease."

Cleibert Bynoe thanked Canon Burton for sharing with him so much of his valuable time and insights. When he left the priest's office, his face beamed with deep appreciation for such an enlivening encounter. He had come to the right place, he said to himself, for this man Burton certainly had a forceful way of explaining what it meant to be Black and Episcopalian in this country. He was, to say the least, extremely impressed with this priest, and it gave him just the measure of discovery which he desired as an explanation of the background and life-force behind such a strong and vibrant Black church as St. Martha's. Burton, he learned, had been trained at a White seminary, with no exposure to Black professors, nor Black authored texts in his theological courses, nor Black parish training in his field education programs.

He had picked up whatever he could from other senior Black fellow-clergy, and had been fortunate enough to visit one or two countries in

Africa, several Caribbean islands, and a few mixed congregations in England which, although led by White priests, were mainly supported by Blacks from the West Indies and Africa on Sunday mornings. Someone had suggested to Burton on one of his three visits to England that if the West Indians stayed at home one Sunday morning, most of the Anglican churches in London would have no congregation that day. English people did not generally go to church, he had learned, for in British history and culture, the Church of England belonged to them, they did not necessarily belong to it. After all, wasn't the Queen the Supreme Governor, or Head, or whatever, of the Church of England? Had not Henry VIII clinched that deal centuries ago?

Burton himself had been appointed an honorary canon of a Cathedral in an African diocese, and this office required that he would seek out material and other forms of assistance in this country for the relief of his African counterparts in that diocese. In addition to being an advocate for those committed to his pastoral care in Miami, therefore, Burton also had to care for those who lived, not in only Miami, but also on the other side of the Atlantic in the Mother Country. For Burton, Cleibert had discovered, it was more important for him to being in service of the Mother Country as an African than to be in allegiance with the Mother Church as an Anglican. However, to be an Afro-Anglican in Miami, as rector of a church as impressive as St. Martha's was, in Cleibert Bynoe's estimation, a most significant contribution to the life and image of the Anglican Communion as a whole. Cleibert therefore left Miami the next day for Baltimore, by an American airline, still feeling very satisfied that to be Black and Anglican was neither contradictory nor confusing, but challenging and exciting, even in America. Yet, he mused to himself, this was all part of what it meant to belong to the Big Church.

He had chosen Baltimore as the second leg of his pilgrimage because he had read much about its history and its prominence as a center of American culture and religious history. He was astonished to learn that there were as many as thirty-nine Episcopal churches in Baltimore, most of them White, of course, although the city itself was predominantly Black. He had also learned that Maryland was a very strong center for Roman Catholicism, and that Jews gave a very good account of themselves as far as numbers were concerned. Where would he find most Blacks? Baltimore was a city of innumerable churches, he was told before-hand, so that he would find hundreds of Black Baptist, Church of God, Pentecostal, and Methodist churches in this city.

However, since he was only focusing on Black Episcopalians this time around, he was anxious to visit one prominent Black congregation which would give him a feel for the type of Anglicanism he expected to find. Cleibert Bynoe was strongly urged to visit St. Alphaeus' Church in Baltimore, for there he would certainly be exposed to a fine demonstration of Black Anglicanism at work at a number of levels - preaching, liturgy, music, youth activities, social outreach, missionary enterprises, ecumenical initiatives, political advocacy, national religious leadership, and evangelical fervor. He was not disappointed.

Having arrived in Baltimore after an uneventful flight, and after a surprisingly ample meal on that American airline, Cleibert immediately got in touch with the Rector of St. Alphaeus, Father Richard Benson. He had written to Father Benson from Barbados informing him of his intended visit and the time of his arrival. This made it easier for him to arrange visits to the church before the coming Sunday morning, as well as an interview with the Rector himself, and some of the leading parishioners. He had heard much about Father Benson and his popularity as an effective preacher, a consummate pastor, and an influential religious leader in Baltimore. He was therefore anxious to meet this famous cleric in the flesh.

As he waited for the priest to arrive for his appointment with him that Friday morning, Cleibert used the opportunity to browse around the church to observe what he could of the similarities and differences between his home church in Barbados, and this rather large gothic edifice in the heart of the city of Baltimore. The name of the patron saint, Alphaeus, was strange to him; but he was well prepared for many strange factors in American religious practices and traditions. The table of the back of the church was packed with a wide variety of literature - pamphlets, announcements, fliers advertising sales and meetings, jobs and trips, reports from various church organizations, left-over bulletins from the previous Sunday, one or two hair-clips and bows, obviously left there or found in the church, as well as an assortment of collection-boxes and offering envelopes for fund-raising ventures. One look at that table was enough to convince Cleibert that this was a parish of action, if the range of material on display was anything to go by.

The interior of the church was brightly decorated, with most of the windows depicting the lives of famous Black persons in American history - Absalom Jones, Martin Luther King Jr., Sojourner Truth, Harriet Tubman, Alexander Crummell, and another personality whose picture surprised Cleibert. It was a painting of Simon of Cyrene. It was surprising to him because he had never associated Simon of Cyrene with Blackness. Indeed, apart from the Ethiopian eunuch mentioned in the Acts of the Apostles, Cleibert Bynoe, with all his formal theological knowledge and lifelong study of things sacred and scriptural, had never realized that there were other Blacks mentioned in the Bible, or that the man who helped Jesus to bear his Cross up to Calvary was a Black man, Simon of Cyrene.

His interview with Father Benson was very informative, although it took him quite some time to get accustomed to the fact that the priest, who had every physical vestige of being White - hair, nose, skin, ears, voice, and lips - claimed to be Black. As far as Cleibert was concerned, he knew a White person when he saw one, and this priest aptly qualified, in his estimation, for such an ethnic designation. During their ninety-minute conversation, however, Father Benson very graciously explained to this Barbadian visitor, that here in America, Blackness was more that just skin tone. Anyone who had even one percent of Black blood in them was considered Black, and there were no gray areas of ethnic mix.

One could not be considered part-Black and part-White in this country. One percent of Black blood was enough to "disqualify" you from any claims to Whiteness. This piece of American demographic explanation troubled Cleibert somewhat, even to the point where he wondered why it never was that the same percentage of White blood in a Black person could "qualify" them to be White. He had quickly chided himself for encouraging such a futile insight, for there could never be any circumstance in America, as far as he could see, where such a principle of ethnic classification could be reversed or even extended.

From his conversation with Father Benson, then, as well as his visits to three group meetings and two Choir rehearsals at St. Alphaeus, Cleibert found himself more than ready to join with the congregation for their regular worship on the Sunday morning. In several respects, St. Alphaeus in Baltimore was quite different from St. Martha's in Miami, although they were both Black Episcopal churches. Chief among the differences was the fact that most of the congregation here in Baltimore were African Americans, with fewer ties to the Caribbean or Africa, with Baptist and Methodist traditions in their background. They had strong leanings towards greater participation in the social and political processes of the city and the State of Maryland, and with a heightened sense of the need to confront the White power structures which were systemically opposed to making room for Blacks at the top.

Here, immigration concerns were never raised openly, except where there was an increased awareness of the Korean and Hispanic sectors of Baltimore apparently making in-roads into traditionally Black areas of commerce and social access. Here too, there was talk of many more social organizations - sororities, fraternities, lodges, social clubs, interest groups, political action caucuses and ecumenical connections - all pointing in the same direction of Black solidarity and progress.

In many ways, Cleibert Bynoe came closer to the stark recognition that the Black Church in Baltimore was, at the very least, the major engine for social information and political action. The worship and work of the church for people of all classes and ages, was clearly to be understood within this framework. That was not to say that the greater glory of God was upstaged, for Cleibert had often heard it said that while Black people strove in many ways to find themselves on God's side, White people were often at pains to demonstrate that God was on their side. He felt very deeply in this context the forces of adversity in the wider society, which so gravely affected the dignity for which every Black Anglican should be striving. These forces had to be confronted with the strong combination of prayer and praise; joined strategically with civic protest, social practice and political prudence. In other words,

Cleibert, said to himself, these people really took to heart the injunction of Jesus in the Gospel that Christians, especially oppressed Christians, had to be wise as serpents while being harmless as doves.

So while the worship experience on that Sunday morning at St. Alphaeus was lively, Spirit-filled, fast-moving, and very energizing, he also appreciated the fact that each liturgical event, such as this, was reinforced by a very electrifying sermon from Father Benson. This gave these people exactly what they needed to go back into the city of Baltimore and its surrounding highways and hedges and fight boldly against the American modern versions of the world, the flesh, and the devil. This is precisely how Father Benson and many of the members had explained it to him, and this was exactly how he himself felt, as he made his way back to his hotel early that Sunday afternoon after the service. With Miami and Baltimore providing him with such vivid, yet contrasting experiences, therefore, he was now more excited to move on to the "City of Brotherly Love", Philadelphia, on the following Thursday.

The ride to Philadelphia on the train was a very pleasant experience for Cleibert Bynoe. It was his first train ride ever, since locomotive transportation had long been abandoned in his native Barbados, after the decline of the sugar-cane plantation system nearly a century before. He was able to reflect on what he had witnessed at St. Alphaeus, and on the many ways in which he found himself being impressed by the vitality and fellowship at that church. He reflected on the large numbers of young children and teenagers who seemed to take special delight in their participation in the life of the church. He was struck by the apparent dedication of so many men who served as mentors and guidance counselors for the young boys. He was encouraged by the high visibility of the women in the leadership of the church, including the presence of the female priest who assisted at the Eucharist that previous Sunday. That happened to be his first experience of worshipping with a female priest, since women were not yet being ordained in Barbados.

More particularly, however, Cleibert made a very careful mental note of what he considered to be the theological undergirding of the life and witness of the Black Episcopalians in Baltimore. Here they were caught up in making sure that the church was a force to be reckoned with in the city, even if it meant inviting the Rector to several social gatherings and political strategy meetings. It was an aspect of the life of the Black Church which demonstrated to him in no uncertain terms that the church had to be the voice of the voiceless, the name of the nameless, the power of the powerless, the hope of the hopeless, and the friend of the friendless. He had heard it put like this during a conversation with one of the lay leaders in the congregation the previous Saturday.

Baltimore had assured Cleibert that Afro-Anglican congregations were much more than assemblies of worship and witness. They were also gatherings of concerned citizens, who also happened to be lively Christians, who were not prepared to abandon the plight of the poor and the under-privileged. It reminded him so powerfully of the description of the church which had been attributed to the late Archbishop William Temple, namely, that the church was an institution which existed primarily for the benefit of those who were not its members.

His visit to St. Alphaeus also assured him that the strength of the Black Church in America was characterized mainly by the reality of human suffering and hope. People stuck to the church in order to keep in touch with some sense of the Divine. They stuck to the church in order to discover for themselves and their own people some sense of belonging and social definition. They stuck to the church for some sense of encouragement and determination in confronting the many challenges of being Black and American at the same time. Indeed, the rector of St. Alphaeus had put a difficult question to his members that last Sunday. It went like this: "Which are you first, are you an American, a Black person, a Black Anglican, or a Christian? Some people find it very difficult to be Black, American, and Christian, all at the same time." This utterance from the pulpit had caused Cleibert no little concern, but as he read the daily newspaper on the train that morning, and gleaned story after story about the plight of Blacks across "the land of the free and the home of the brave", he came to a less uncomfortable understanding of what Father Benson had been preaching about.

In Philadelphia, he was immediately fascinated by the sense of history which seemed to dominate the city. He had read much about the prominence of this town from many sources, and he had seen pictures of some of the famous sites, such as the Liberty Bell, and the place where the American Congress first met. He was deeply touched by his visit to St. George's Methodist Church, out of which Richard Allen and Absalom Jones had been ejected more than two centuries ago. He was moved, too, by the spectacles of hundreds of Blacks on the streets of the city who seemed to have no jobs, no homes, no friends, and no hope.

It touched him deeply and made him aware that although he was visiting the richest country in the world, he was still observing some of the poorest conditions he had ever experienced. There was nothing in Barbados with which to compare what he was seeing here. All this he tried to relate to the life and witness of the Anglican church in general, and the Afro-Anglican church. Above all, it prepared him for what he would experience at St. Didymus' Church that following Sunday, on this the third leg of his Anglican pilgrimage to America. He really belonged to the Big Church, and the variations of church life that he saw made it real.

The Church of St. Didymus was in an unusual place. It was a Black church located in a predominantly White neighborhood of Philadelphia. The members were generally from outside the area, and in some instances, they had to travel a considerable distance to get there. Cleibert had observed this as a general pattern in his visit so far. The people came from far, and rarely from nearby, to attend church. This was quite different from his own situation in Barbados, where most of the members of his home church lived close to the church. It gave him a sense of respect for the efforts which many people, especially those who did not have their own means of transportation, made to assemble for worship in their special house of God.

The Eucharist at St. Didymus followed the same pattern as the others. However, it did not take Cleibert long to observe that many of the members of this congregation were of a lighter complexion, more elegantly dressed than those at St. Alphaeus, and generally exuding a type of bearing which suggested a certain air of sophistication. This was tempered however by the high level of energy which they exhibited throughout the service. There was the wearing of kente cloths by the choir, the acolytes, the ushers, and the Sunday School teachers. There were the spontaneous ejaculations of praise, affirmations and testimony during the sermon and the prayers. There was the use of the Afro-American Hymnal, *Lift Every Voice And Sing II,* which he had heard about, but which he was now using for the very first time.

There was much in the liturgical experience here which gave him the distinct impression that many of the members had not been Anglicans all of their lives, but had brought over into Anglican worship some of the liturgical habits and styles inherited from the evangelical modes of worship. Cleibert was singularly impressed. He called this a mark of the Spirit, and later spoke about it to the Rector, Father Mathis, when they met for a brief consultation after the service.

Father Mathis was very gracious in his conversation with the Barbadian, and welcomed the opportunity to share some insights with him not only about life at St. Didymus, a very historic church in the story of Black Episcopalianism, but also a very important place of worship for some of the movers and shakers in the Black community here in Philadelphia. He asserted that the church was not just a social gathering, even if the people appeared to be so warm and friendly, and fellowship oriented. It was for them a place of recharging; a place where they could gather some more strength for dealing with the realities of life in Philadelphia. For, life was very hard for Blacks; and the Church was there to provide for them, not a place of escape, but rather a springboard for engagement in the total process.

Here at St. Didymus, although the worship of God came first, and although he tried to hold up before them their obligations as faithful Christians who were in duty bound to worship God in Spirit and in truth, he was also responsive to their needs and aspirations as full citizens of a land of opportunities, many of which were being denied them because of their race. At St. Didymus, he said, there was networking, and fellowship-making, and resource-sharing, and extended family, and hospital, and schooling, and social affirmation, and a peace-loving shelter from many storms in the city caused by drug, alcohol, violence and crime.

Cleibert inquired about an organization which had been mentioned both here and in Baltimore. It was the UBE, the Union of Black Episcopalians; their annual meeting was just weeks away from being held in New Orleans, and notices in the church bulletins, as well as informative fliers, had been urging members not to miss this year's gathering. Mathis explained that this was an organization established years ago which was designed to encourage Blacks in the Episcopal church, especially at a time when they were feeling the pangs of isolation and injustice from the White leadership of the church at both diocesan and national levels. The UBE had provided for its members a haven for reaffirmation and encouragement. It was to be a national instrument of solidarity and cohesion for sharing information and fellowship in the struggle to maintain human dignity and Christian character, especially in a church which still had difficulties in welcoming all of God's people with open arms.

"Is there a union of White Episcopalians?" Cleibert had asked.

"They don't need one!" replied Father Mathis. "The Episcopal Church in this country is nearly ninety percent White, so there you have it!"

It still gave Cleibert some problems to imagine why it was necessary to have a union of Blacks in a Church that was essentially a Black church world-wide. But he was not unaware of the tremendous struggles which were being faced by Black Episcopalians in this country to maintain their sense of belonging and allegiance to the American version of Anglicanism. And it really was an American version for him. But, that was precisely what he had come this country to observe. These realities therefore came together for him in a forceful way, as he arrived in Brooklyn, New York, to spend a few days with his relatives, to attend St. Simon of Cyrene Episcopal Church there, and then to make his way back home to Barbados shortly thereafter.

This visit to his relatives in Brooklyn turned out to be much more than a sort of homecoming for him, meeting with those whom he had not seen for many years. To worship at St. Simon's was like worshipping at his own church back in Barbados, especially as the congregation there was mainly comprised of people from Barbados, Jamaica, Trinidad, and St. Vincent. Cleibert found himself in the middle of the Caribbean diaspora at St. Simon's - accents, laughter, social habits, jokes, folk-sayings, singing, cuisine, attire, and noise - hardly anything was missing from a typical West Indian church gathering. It was essentially like a home away from home. But this was America, not Barbados.

The service was as lively as Cleibert had expected it. Most of the congregation arrived late for the ten-thirty service that morning, as Cleibert had also expected them to. The little children were exquisitely dressed, extremely active in the pews during the service, especially during the sermon. The notices and announcements covered a wide range of concerns and intimations, including opportunities for employment and suggestions for acquiring affordable health care. There were reports on the recent diocesan events with an emphasis on the implications for the parish budget, and the ways in which members would be called on to be more supportive. The hymns in the service were taken from the standard Episcopal Church hymnal, although many of the tunes to which they were sung were taken from the typical Anglican hymnal used in the West Indies, *Hymns Ancient & Modern (Standard Version).*

The singing was lusty and loud, the choir was often overtaken by the congregation, and the organist often gave in to the slow pace of the congregational singing. The people preferred to sing to their hearts' content rather than to the organist's direction. This was church, Cleibert mused to himself, this was church; and although they were thousands of miles away from the native land, it was clear to him that his fellow worshippers were making the most of what they had, where they were, and in their own inimitable way. Not only were they worshipping the Lord in the beauty of holiness, he thought, they were also worshipping the Lord in the holiness of beauty. It was the live face of Anglicanism, Black Anglicanism, and he was grateful for this opportunity to experience some of its richness, so far from his native Barbados.

His visit to New York was such an enthralling experience, far exceeding what he had anticipated. He therefore decided not to take in a visit to Washington on this trip, but to save it for another occasion. He was able to visit several church buildings in Manhattan, to attend a week-day service in the Cathedral of St. John the Divine, where he was struck by the multiplicity of signs and symbols, shops and programs, colors and causes, which all made up the life of that historic house of worship. It was the strangest church building he had ever visited, he said to himself; but he quickly remembered that one preacher had once referred to God as a God of surprises. It should therefore not be too strange, after all, if the house of that same God should be adorned with surprising things. It was a face of Anglicanism with which he was not quite prepared to deal, but still, it was Anglican.

IV

———

C leibert Bynoe finally left New York for Barbados on another BWIA flight. This time, there was no Mormon to converse with; only another Barbadian who was returning home after not having done so for more than twenty years. This gave Cleibert the opportunity to describe the new Barbados to his traveling compatriot, and to warn him that the changes at home would in some instances be hard for him to absorb. The world was changing, and so was Barbados, as conservative as it was often reputed to be. Cleibert had some quiet time to make some summary notes to himself on all that he had encountered on his Anglican pilgrimage. He jotted down the issues with which he understood the Black Anglican congregations in America were most confronted. These included racism, human sexuality, womanhood and religious leadership, class prejudice, ethnocentrism, xenophobia, immigration reform, welfare reform. He also listed resource identification and deployment, diocesan involvement, recruitment of candidates for theological training and ordination. Episcopal involvement in the Black Church in America, theological pluralism and ecumenical cooperation with other denominations could not be left out, he noted. Above all, the challenge of distinguishing the traditions of Anglicanism from the vestiges of the British cultural ethos still had to be addressed globally.

It was his summary description of a typical Afro-Anglican congregation in America, where the membership was predominantly from the Caribbean that comprised most of his notes and occupied his literary imagination. He had gathered a great deal of insights from the many persons with whom he had spoken during his pilgrimage.

This gave him more than enough confidence in composing a profile of a typical congregation that would reflect quite vividly the ecclesial pleasures of exile. It would also assess the spiritual linkages with the native Caribbean. Cleibert took great pains in drawing up the profile of a congregation in America which he named St. Nathaniel's. The profile was quite a detailed characterization of the encounters and experiences he had witnessed and enjoyed during his personal pilgrimage to America.

Cleibert's descriptive profile of St. Nathaniel's Church is outlined in what follows next.

One typical Afro-Anglican congregation in the Episcopal Church is St. Nathaniel's. It is typical of many such congregations. Its address will not be disclosed. It is comprised of a massive assembly of Anglicans who have made America their new home, having migrated from the islands in the Caribbean Basin, or from countries in the South. They have come to America in search of opportunities for survival, growth, and progress. They have brought with them not only a strong determination to succeed, but also a strong attachment to their religious roots and background. They make up the largest sector of Afro-Anglicans in America. They were born Anglican, their parents, grandparents, great-grandparents were all Anglican, and they are determined to remain Anglican, even if the church goes by another name (Episcopal) in this country.

Anglicanism for them is a black experience, very black indeed, for they were born into communities where they were the ethnic majority, and where, in almost every respect, blackness was the color of their reality. Even if they were led by White Englishmen in their pulpits and at their altars, for some of the time, it did not make much of a difference as to who they were or what they espoused, for the pews were all filled with black bodies and black souls anyway.

The ministers may have led the worship in church, but the people have always led the life of the church. Why? This was because the church for them was much more than a place, or an assembly of worship. It was a major social instrument of their cultural life and civic activity. It provided them with a source of civic access, personal engagement, and educational development. It nurtured their sense of family and community belonging. It strengthened their resolve to make the little that they had go a very long way. It provided them with modes of human fulfillment, social uplift, and common exchange. Their church was their life, and their life was in their church. Anglicanism, then, was more than just a denominational movement. It was indeed a principal carrier of their culture, although it had all started in England and had made its way to their shores primarily for the English who, until recently, ruled over them.

But they were now in a new paradise, America. This was the land of their God-given opportunity. Their Anglican heritage would have to be preserved in such a way that their sense of allegiance to the God who had brought them thus far on the way, could be expressed in terms and tones which were deeply rooted in their religious upbringing and basic social outlook. They were now members of St. Nathaniel's. The people of St. Nathaniel's were wedded to the belief that their well-being and progress, spiritual, moral, social, and material, were inextricably linked to their participation in the life of their church. They love their church, even if they are financially unable to support it lavishly. They compensate for their lack of money by offering freely of their time and talents. The limited income which they command has often to be shared by two households – one in America, where they live, and the other in the Islands where their relatives wait for their share from America. Remittances from America are still a major source of revenue in the Caribbean

For them, the church is their main source of contact with their homeland. Sunday mornings for them are like regular trips to their homelands, singing the familiar hymns from that well-known hymnal *Hymns Ancient & Modern*. They are forced to use the other hymnals authorized for use in the Episcopal Church, but they prefer to substitute familiar tunes instead of those provided, wherever possible. They are very selective about the modern American hymns, for they say that most are neither "sweet" nor "sacred". They participate in the rituals and ceremonies that resemble those on which they were nurtured in the islands, as being essential to their liturgical health. They would join in the various and sundry traditional activities of church-life for the sake of the old and the young, the sick and the sickly, the outcasts and the lapsed, the marginalized and the bereaved. Church life for them is a comprehensive panoply of community enrichment. It is all part of belonging to the Big Church.

Yet, Sunday mornings also provide them with an invaluable opportunity for becoming more acquainted with the ways of America, and for exchanging ideas and valuable information. They are informed about the civic duties and social events affecting their homes and families. They are engaged in the building of stronger fellowship (whether Christian, or cultural) in the face of an incessantly hostile and racialized environment. They seek to find new sources of strength to deal the week ahead of them. They offer their prayers and praises to a God who makes a "way out of no way". They intercede for those less fortunate than themselves. They offer advice and consolation to those who have fallen on hard times. They bring their contributions to the common table for sharing with the needy and the socially deprived.

They come together to share in a common parenting of the younger generations in their assemblies. They make common cause with the bands of fellow sufferers who cry out for justice and equality in this the "land of the free and the home of the brave". They are Afro-Anglicans, yes, but they are also persons of African descent in America. They are not African Americans; they are Afro-Caribbeans. They insist on making that distinction, for better or for worse; but especially since the term "Black" has apparently been generally understood as an exclusive synonym for Black people born in America. They know precisely where their higher interests lie, and how much solidarity is required to pursue them. Their active participation in the life of the church, therefore, is critical for the worship of God, their sojourn in America, and their diligence in working for themselves and their future. But who are their leaders?

Their lay leaders are generally those who have been involved in the life of the church from their earliest days. They were acolytes and choristers, teachers and catechists, group leaders and vestrypersons in the Islands. Thus, their participation in the leadership of the church is simply an extension of their upbringing. It gives them a sense of continuity with their home church-life, and it also provides them with the scope and opportunities for making a distinctive contribution to the development of their fellow members. Of course, there are some lay leaders who see their positions as pockets of power, and therefore tend to exercise as much influence as possible in the life of the church, sometimes in competition with the ordained leadership.

But this is not peculiar to the lay leadership of St. Nathaniel's, since there often exists abundant evidence in diocesan conventions to show that the authority of the priest in the parish is likely be challenged by the vocal lay leadership. This happens as much in White parishes as it does in Afro-Anglican congregations. It clearly reflects the political climate and context that governs the secular society. The struggle with democracy in the life of the church is often brought under the judgment of the nature of the church itself, in which there is to be One Lord, One Faith, One Baptism, One God and Parent of us all.

The ordained leadership at St. Nathaniel's is often peopled by Afro-Caribbean clergy who were trained for the priesthood outside of the United States. Most of them would have been trained either at Codrington College in Barbados, or at the United Theological College of the West Indies (UTCWI) in Jamaica. The general scenarios would have been that they migrated to America to further their studies, fell in love with the country as a whole, or fell out of favor with their bishops in the Islands, and then decided to remain in America permanently. But there are those who would have been recruited by parishes for specific appointments in the Episcopal Church, as well as those who would have made a deliberate choice to migrate to America in search of better opportunities for themselves and their families.

Their reasons for coming to America are generally no different from all the Irish, or British, or other Europeans who also migrate in greater numbers, all in search of better opportunities. The unfortunate fact is that they are often asked by the Americans why they have left their own homes, with a frequency that is not addressed to the White immigrants from Europe or elsewhere. But they are usually convinced that God has brought them to this country, if only to minister to their own people, at such a time as this.

Some of the clergy at St. Nathaniel's, however, are African Americans, born in this country. They would have been trained at Episcopal seminaries mainly by White professors and instructors. Their seminary programs would normally be devoid of much practical exposure to the life and work of the Anglican Church beyond these shores. Nevertheless, some of them would have made occasional visits to the Caribbean, or Africa, to familiarize themselves with the places and congregational cultures from which many of their members have come.

In the wider society, there have been persistent tensions between West Indians in America and African Americans, based mainly on a general failure of each sector to understand each other's historical struggles and cultural backgrounds. These tensions are generally suppressed in Afro-Anglican congregations, such as St. Nathaniel's primarily through the spirit of openness and inter-cultural bonding which membership in the church usually generates. Thus, Black History Month and Homecoming are just as popular on the liturgical calendar of St. Nathaniel's as are the Harvest festivals and the Patronal festivals, to which persons from the Islands are accustomed.

What is of critical importance for the life of St. Nathaniel's, however, is that the clergy provide for the membership that source of leadership, moral mentorship, pastoral guidance, and civic advocacy. They often perform functions as legal counsel, foster parenting, elder brother/sister, or special sounding-board, which the members treasure beyond words. There often exists among clergy and laity that solid bond of friendship and common pilgrimage that can withstand many of the social and material pressures that are part and parcel of the test of living in America. Many of them would readily admit that it takes a great amount of faith in God to live in America, especially as life often appears to be so fragile, fortunes so fickle, and families so vulnerable.

St. Nathaniel's provides for many persons a type of "security blanket" (as some have actually described their church membership), and their sense of belonging in the community is reinforced by their sense of allegiance to God through their active participation in the worship and life of the church. "Church" for them is much more an active verb than it is a noun. The people of St. Nathaniel's *do* church, they do not merely *go to* church. Whether it is the annual excursion or banquet, whether it is the frequent funeral or occasional wedding, whether it is the "christening" (baptism) of another baby born to a member, or the graduation of one of their bright sons/daughters, the whole church comes alive in an extended family celebration. But the question might well be asked: Is this what Anglicanism is to be all about? Is this the exotic face of the Episcopal Church, or does this quality of church life have its proper place within *Ecclesia Anglicana* here in America? It all depends on who provides the answer to this question. They all belong to "Big Church".

This final issue was critical for Cleibert himself, since he was now on his way back to his native Barbados, which was otherwise known as Little England, and where Anglicans were once nicknamed "Black Englishmen". There was a danger, he felt, in not making the necessary distinction between what was essentially Anglican and what was culturally British. For, as he had observed in some of what he encountered in America, White Episcopalians seemed quite comfortable with the blurring of that distinction. For Cleibert Bynoe, however, to be Black and Anglican was a struggle especially in America, he only hoped that his fellow Anglicans in that country would avoid any attempts to be both Black and British.

After all, this was America wasn't it? And the main thrust of being American and Episcopalian was to establish a separate identity with all the implications of independence and freedom which such a distinction required. In any event, he said to himself as the final approach to landing in Barbados was announced, he was not a member of the British Empire any longer, he was a member of the Anglican Communion - non-British, non-White, non-monolithic the Big Church indeed! As long as every Anglican congregation remembered that, and sought to live out its challenges and demands, the world would see and know that Anglicans in America, whether Black, White or brown, were indeed integral members of the one, holy, catholic, and apostolic church. They all belong to Big Church!

Section Three

Soundings in Caribbean Anglicania

Sermon Preached at the Consecration

Of

The Reverend Sehon Goodridge

As

The Bishop of the Windward Islands

St. George's Cathedral, Kingstown, St. Vincent

December 7th, 1994

For we can no longer escape from the duty of teaching which the needs of the priesthood have laid upon us, though we tried to avoid it.... And this very thing I desire, so that in the endeavour to teach, I may be able to learn. For one is the true Master, Who alone has not learnt, what He taught all; but men learn before they teach, and receive from Him what they may hand on to others. Therefore I must learn and teach at the same time." (St. Ambrose, **On The Duties Of The Clergy**, Bk1, Chap 1:2,3,4).

These are excerpts from one of St. Ambrose's most famous treatises, and they reflect the measure of the man whose consecration as the Bishop of Milan took place 1620 years ago today, December 7,374. In more than one respect, Sehon Goodridge is a modern-day Ambrose. Both share the same anniversary date of consecration. Neither of them was on the original slate of candidates for episcopal election. They differ in their response to their election, however. Ambrose, the 35-year-old Governor of Liguria and Aemillia was not yet baptized when he was elected by popular acclamation, "Ambrose bishop!" He quickly went into hiding because he did not want to be a bishop, but his friend Leontius handed him over to the church. On the other hand, I have heard of no such reluctance on Canon

Goodridge's part; he has been regarded as a bishop-in-the-making for the last two decades!

As a bishop, Ambrose saw himself primarily as a teacher; the office of the bishop was to teach. He embraced a simplicity of life, and disposed of all his wealth, except for what he needed to secure the welfare of his sister. He went heavily into the study of the Scriptures and other leading thinkers of his day. He gave himself over to hard work, refused to attend cocktail parties, entertained his guests very frugally, and made himself readily accessible to his flock. He strongly favored the life of consecrated virgins, many of whom came under his direction. But many mothers refused to allow their daughters to listen to his sermons, for he was accused of trying to depopulate the empire. Ambrose replied that it was wars, not virgins that destroyed the human race.

He confronted the rulers of his day in their excessive use of power, insisting that "The emperor is in the church, not over it." It is generally believed that it was his life, character and teaching that was mainly responsible for the conversion of that great African saint, Augustine of Hippo. Augustine spoke of Ambrose as "a faithful teacher of the Church, and even at the risk of his life a most strenuous defender of Catholic truth." He wrote many books, preached every Sunday and holy day, composed many hymns, and championed the cause of the poor. He died on Good Friday 397, and was buried on Easter Day. Thus, with Augustine, Jerome, and Gregory the Great, Ambrose has come down to us as one of the four doctors of the Latin Church. A doctor is primarily a teacher. A bishop is a doctor in the Church.

Today, as a community of believers who share in the same catholic and apostolic tradition of Ambrose and Augustine, we meet in the fellowship of God's Spirit, to set apart yet another Shepherd, another pastor, another doctor, another teacher, another chief servant in the household of God. It is another defining moment in the ever-unfolding pilgrimage of our church. It is rich with history and sacred gossip, packed with meaning and ecclesial memories, filled with hopes and glorious uncertainties, garnished with sweet smells and melodious bells, heralded with modern rites and ancient ceremonies. Yet another bishop has been chosen to lead the flock of Christ in this Diocese.

The Church in the Province of the West Indies gathers together in Hairouna, the old name for St. Vincent, to give open witness to what it proclaims as God's mission, God's way forward. Thus, by solemn prayer and corporate laying-on-of-hands, the bishops here assembled give sacramental expression, on God's behalf and ours, to our highest expectations for this man of God. For after the noises of our solemn assemblies have ceased, and the friendly feet and faces from abroad have retired, the new bishop will be left alone with his faithful people around him to continue to be the church, to perfect the work of ministry, to proclaim by word, witness, and example, not only the liberating truth of the Gospel of Christ, but also its radically transforming and convulsive effect.

My dear friends, I would invite you to consider with me two very critical questions for the lasting sanctity and missionary impact of this historic occasion. First, what lessons can Ambrose still teach the members of this Diocese – Bishop, priests, and people? Second, what word can we leave with the new bishop, as he begins his lovely, yet lonely, task in God's vineyard? The concerns of Christians in Georgetown, St. Vincent, are not all that different from those in Georgetown, Guyana, or Georgetown, Washington, D.C. Our Gospel reading for today is a reminder that Jesus has come to bring life to us in all its fullness. Some people still call it "abundant life".

What does it mean to have abundant life? Are there human concerns for abundant living which do not affect what it means to be a faithful follower of Jesus Christ in the modern world? I can think of none whatsoever. In other words, all sheep eat from the same grass whether we are Christian or not. But the basic issue has to do with how Christians deal with the common forces of life which affect our human condition. None of us Christians can afford to be so heavenly that we are of no earthly use. This is surely what the Church means by Incarnation. So, what are these forces which affect our human condition? Ambrose would suggest that they are threefold: Wealth, Power, and Justice.

When we hear these terms mentioned we are undoubtedly driven to think of them in the most common of ways: wealth is what you acquire. Power is what you exercise, and justice is that for which you struggle. Yet both Ambrose and today's readings from the Bible point us in a different direction. There can be no doubt that our Caribbean region continues to experience increasing levels of poverty. Far from there being much wealth to accumulate, there is an even more pitiful spectacle of the distribution of the wealth available. The haves and the have-nots live side by side in painful, and sometimes blissful, contempt of each other.

One prominent Vincentian priest Canon Leopold Baynes, was recently in Washington preaching at an Independence Celebration Eucharist at my church and describing some areas of need among poor children here in this country. I am happy to report that his words bore some fruit, and that eight barrels of supplies are arriving here shortly from Washington, via New York, from my church congregation and the Vincentian community in the Washington area. But although eight barrels cannot solve the problems of poverty anywhere, they can point to an important lesson from the four Gospels and the teachings of Ambrose.

I refer, of course, to the miracle story of the feeding of the five thousand, which, apart from the resurrection of Jesus, is the only miracle story recorded in all four Gospels. The great miracle of sharing tells us plainly about the Christian attitude to wealth. It is to be an attitude of appreciation through sharing what you have, and not of accumulation through procuring what you do not have. This is how Ambrose puts it: "He who sent the apostles without gold also brought together the churches without gold. The Church has gold, not to store up, but to lay out, and to spend on those who need". When you ask Ambrose to define the real wealth of the church, he turns to St. Lawrence. He relates the story of Lawrence being ordered by the civil authorities to produce the treasures of the church. Lawrence promised to produce them by the following day. When the authorities came to collect the wealth, Lawrence assembled all the poor people of the church in front of them and said, "These are the treasures of the Church!"

The challenge for us as Caribbean Christians is to appreciate the invaluable wealth of who we are, the enormous potential of the little that we know we have, and the surprising limits of what we really need. In the context of our material condition, the Christian Gospel challenges us towards a radical appreciation of the vast wealth of our other resources – productive creativity, survival skills, cultural imagination, spiritual fortitude, social courage, and the tastes for freedom – just to name a few. These are the elements of our Caribbean wealth that no amount of money, whether foreign or domestic, can buy for us. It is for us to take the lead in the Church, by what we say and how we witness, that neither these resources, nor ourselves, will ever be for sale. It is for us to come to see more clearly, that despite what we see on TV, or bring back from the North, the verb TO BE is infinitely more important than the verb TO HAVE. Nobody has put it better for us than an 84-year-old woman in Haiti (Carmen Jean Gilles) when she said: "We have so little, and we believe in so much."

The appreciation of the five barley loaves and two small fish to feed five thousand is incredibly more precious than the accumulation of 5000 loaves and 2000 fish to feed seven people. Through the sacramental life of sharing, the Gospel of Jesus Christ teaches us how to do more with less. We must learn as we teach and teach as we learn.

Then there is the issue of power, which, like fire, can easily be described as a good servant and a bad master. It is the relentless struggle for power and its mindless abuse across the globe, through various demonic policies and systems, which constitutes the essential face of evil in the modern world. The power of gold and dope is often outmatched by the power of the bomb and the bullet; and both are often silenced by the power of death. It gives me no joy whatever to acknowledge that, for many of our younger generation, the culture of death carries far more power for them than the promise of life.

The image of the Good Shepherd which we have in today's Gospel gives us the clue to the whole power-question in Christian thinking and discourse. The Good Shepherd is also the Door, and the Bread of Life, and the True Vine, and the Way, the truth, and the Life, and the Light of the World, and the Resurrection and the Life. All these images radiate from the one man who said that he came that others might have abundant life, that is, life in all its fullness. So, the Good Shepherd is the enabler, and he is in the life-giving business, and the power which he has is only valid and valuable because it is in the life-giving service of others.

We live in a world where people seek power, and if they cannot gain it fairly then they seize it. Yet we also belong to a community of faith. It is a community of mutual enablement, in which people are baptized and sent out to give power – the power to believe, the power to think, the power to love, the power to hope, the power to forgive, the power to emancipate, the power to care for those who care little for us, the power to celebrate the grace of God in all its mystical and matchless splendor. It is the power of the Spirit, and that of no other.

In the Church we are members together of the community of the Spirit, that Spirit of God to whom we will shortly pray in solemn tones before the act of ordination. The community of the Spirit is also the community of spiritual gifts – the "charismata". God's Spirit empowers the whole church by making available to us varieties of charisms. We must notice how our common language sometimes associates the word "charisma" even with strange and debilitating forms of power. We like to speak of leaders in the public sphere as charismatic leaders, by which we mean that they draw people to themselves by outstanding acts of persuasion. It is time for the Church of Christ, in this and every place, to take back the word "charisma" from those who have seized it, and to give courageous and concrete expression to it as that which we derive from our life in the Spirit. It is about the distribution of power, and not about the control of it. This is what we mean when we pray in our Eucharist: "May we upon whom your Spirit shines give light to the world". We must teach as we learn and learn as we teach.

The third issue is that of Justice, a word that is often used so glibly, a virtue that is often observed in its breach, an ideal towards which we often grow tired in our striving. It is the message of Second-Isaiah in our first Reading for today which brings it fresh before our notice. We find it in what is known as the second Servant Song. God's chosen servant, God's anointed, will bring forth justice to the people, faithfully, continuously, and courageously. He cannot give up. He will not give up, and neither shall he fail. The justice of which Isaiah speaks is identical with God's character; it is God's righteousness.

Isaiah goes on to remind us that the servant is given by God as a covenant, a solemn bond, a binding contract, to the people to bring light to those in darkness, and sight to those who cannot see, and emancipation to those imprisoned by various forms of bondage. In other words, he does not say what justice is, he is only concerned with what justice does. To use an African-American expression, it is not how you talk the talk, but how you walk the walk. The Church cannot expect to be taken seriously about its demands for justice in the marketplace if it fails to take seriously God's demands for justice within its own sacred space. For wherever people are oppressed and excluded because of the way God made them – whether tall or short, fat or thin, male or female, light or dark, native or foreigner – then the church, as the servant community, in sacred covenant with God, comes under the divine judgment of the very justice it seeks to proclaim.

Ambrose enters again; and he waxes eloquent on the pre-eminence of justice in the life of the Christian. As is well known, justice is listed with courage, temperance, and prudence as the four cardinal virtues. Ambrose makes a very close link between prudence and justice. He says: "Justice cannot exist without prudence, since it demands no small amount of prudence to see whether a thing is just or unjust... Nor, on the other hand, can prudence exist without justice, for piety towards God is the beginning of understanding." (Bk.1, Ch XXVII, 126). He says that justice and goodwill hold a society together, for the one gives judgment and the other gives goodness. But then Ambrose, the Christian teacher, goes all the way. He says that the foundation of justice is faith – your faith and mine, which we have in Christ (or, at least, we claim to have). Listen to Ambrose again: "For Christ is the object of faith to all; but the Church is as it were the outward form of justice, she is the common right of all. For all in common she prays, for all in common she works, in the temptations of all she is tried." (Bk1. Ch.XX1X,142).

Can you imagine what life would be like if all members of the church could say with Ambrose that the church is the outward form of justice? Just think of the consequences for relationships of all kinds -for bishops and clergy, clergy and parishioners, young and old, vestry-members and sextons. Think of the new hopes that would be generated among those who are- frustrated and hopelessly marginalized! Think of the many who would return to our fold with renewed faith and passionate vigor! Think of the dormant resources that could be trapped, or the many gifts, talents, and vocations that could be brought to their fullness. Yes, the church would then begin to be about its Father's business, namely, the celebration of divine justice, and not merely its proclamation. We are always to seek first the kingdom of God and God's righteousness before we get worked up about other things of lesser importance.

Wealth, Power, and Justice, these are the critical forces for the Church's mission which Paul, John, Isaiah, and Ambrose, would bring before our notice today. They call us to the sacramental appreciation of our wealth. They call us to the radical distribution of God's power, God's life-giving presence in our midst. They call us to the renewed celebration of justice. But in doing so they remind us that each force has its darker side, where sin and evil hold sway. For wealth is beset by greed; power is distorted by its abuse; and justice is denied by poor judgment. Every servant of God, whether ordained or lay, must be sober and vigilant, lest these roaring lions devour the flock of Christ. Ambrose puts it this way: "We know that contempt of riches is a form of justice, therefore we ought to avoid love of money, and strive with all our powers never to do anything against justice, but to guard it in all our deeds and actions." (Bk.11, Ch.XXVII,133). Let us learn as we teach; and let us teach as we learn.

Allow me, then, dear friends to share with Sehon, my friend and brother in the Lord, a few reflections for his pilgrimage. Sehon, just over thirty years ago when we were both students at Codrington College, you, Lionel Crawford and I were walking up the College drive one evening, complaining about some mini crisis in the College. You suddenly lifted your hands to heaven and shouted, "God come for your world, boy!" I have come here to tell you today that, in this service, God is continuing to answer your prayer through your own self. You will have to be careful about what you ask for, you might just get it!

Again, Sehon, during the course of your distinguished career you have accomplished many things. Many honors have come your way. You have been granted so many honorary titles: doctor, canon, chaplain, fellow. You will no doubt remember that I once called you "the honorarium"! But Sehon, you cannot be an honorary bishop. This ordination is for real. The sheep of Christ in this place are waiting to be led by their new shepherd. What mode of shepherding do you plan to adopt? I do not need to be persuaded that you have well weighed and pondered these things long before this time!

Permit me to say this, my dear brother. Because we have been reflecting on wealth, power, and justice, you might have been tempted to make a mental and theological connection with John Calvin's triple office of Christ as prophet, priest and king. But let me remind you that you are not Calvinist, you are Anglican! Let me therefore urge you to connect the triple office of Christ with what the four Gospels tell us about him. They say that Jesus was a Preacher, a Teacher, and a Healer. The preaching and the healing will give you few problems, for God and the Bible will help you; but the teaching will give you many. You will have to teach as you understand and understand what you really believe. You will have to teach by your words, your witness, and your public and private example. You will certainly have to teach as you learn and learn as you teach. You must remain fully assured that God's gracious and enlivening Spirit will always be available to guide you, as long as you open yourself wide enough, and long enough to receive.

So, let me put my mouth right inside your business before I come down, for I may never have a chance to do it again!

First, expect martyrdom with the miter. Martyrdom and "Miterdom" always go together. Do you remember all that talk about "altar of sacrifice"? Well, Sehon, this is it! Do not be dismayed when your hand is bitten by the same mouths it feeds; or when you are misunderstood, or misrepresented by those who should know better, and do better. All bishops suffer that way! So, you will have plenty of company.

Second, now that you are leaving us on the outside, and going into the house of bishops, do not forget to open the windows a little wider when you get in. Many of us faithful sheep want to know what our shepherds talk and joke about, what they fuss about, what causes them pain, or what really makes them happy. We want to eavesdrop on their lives a little more, not for the gossip, but for the Gospel. So, try and bring them a little closer to us by opening the windows in the house. We want to be able to discern more clearly that our humanity and theirs is the same, in spite of the zucchettos and miters, the purple socks and the golden staffs. We love our bishops; and we want to know them better.

Third, do not fool yourself that your people are only connected with one god, regardless of what they say in the creeds of the Church. You have enough experience in the Caribbean and Britain to know that it is not really so. Find out who the other gods are, Sehon, by listening carefully to what your clergy and people say, and by watching closely for the other altars at which they also worship. Life is so hard and complex, Sehon, that most people practice the belief that two gods or more are better than one. This is not a Haitian problem; this is a widespread human practice.

As a bishop, you must try to avoid confrontation between the God of Jesus and other gods. Rather, you must try to generate a conversation between them. You see, the confrontation is already taking place in the very hearts and lives of your people, deep in the recesses of their soul. They are looking for someone to teach them how to turn their inner confrontation into a purposeful conversation, for such conversations can often lead to sincere repentance and genuine conversion.

Fourth, I trust that you do not intend to limit yourself to being a *pastor pastorum*, a pastor of pastors. I trust rather that you will encompass the vision of becoming a *pastor fidelium*, a pastor of all the faithful. But you must also be a friend, not a prelate. Ambrose says, "He cannot be friend to a man who has been unfaithful to God. Friendship is the guardian of pity and the teacher of equality, so as to make the superior equal to the inferior, and the inferior to the superior." (Bk.111. Ch.XX11,132) This means, among other things, Sehon, that you must be a pastorly friend, and not just a friendly pastor. Friendliness is cheap, but friendship is costly. The late Father Jenson warned us years ago in College that the adjective "popular" should never describe the noun "priest". I believe that goes for bishops too!

So, listen finally to the Risen Jesus as he teases your spirit of faith to send you on your mission and ministry. Sehon, King of the Amorites, do you love me more than these? Feed my lambs! Sehon, son of Simon

Goodridge, do you love me more than these! Tend my sheep! Sehon, bishop in my church, do you love me more than these! Feed my sheep! What he is simply saying to you, my dear Brother, is this: Love the People! Love the People! Love the People! And may God's richest grace always be with you. AMEN

Sermon preached at the Consecration of

The Rev. Robert Thompson

As

The Bishop Suffragan of Kingston

Kingston Parish Church, Kingston, Jamaica

Tuesday May 31, 2005

"Let the word of Christ dwell in you richly; teach and admonish one another in all wisdom; and with gratitude in your hearts sing psalms, hymns, and spiritual songs to God. And whatever you do, in word or deed, do everything in the name of the Lord Jesus, giving thanks to God the Father through him." (Colossians 3:16-17) (RSV)

My Dear Sisters and Brothers in the Lord, I wonder if you ever noticed that Christianity has always been a very fashion-conscious religion. It has always placed a great emphasis on clothes. I am not referring so much to our cultural habits of turning our Sunday morning services into fashion parades, especially at Easter, or Harvest, or Christmas. Indeed, for many people, churchgoing can be a very expensive affair that some people just cannot afford – if for no other reason than they do not want to be seen in the same clothes too often. No, I am really referring to Christianity's origins, and its history, and to its symbolic teachings about clothing. Clothes are mentioned everywhere. Clothes often get featured in the reports and the teachings, in the rituals and ceremonies, the symbolisms and styles.

For example, we know what the Baby Jesus wore as soon as he was born – it wasn't pampers; it wasn't a diaper; but just swaddling-cloths, or if you prefer the King James version, "swaddling clothes". On the Mount of Transfiguration his clothes are mentioned in dramatic fashion – they become dazzling White. Just before his final walk to

Calvary the Roman soldiers adorned him in a scarlet robe, and put a crown of thorns on his head, and mocked him. We know what he was wearing just before he was stripped for crucifixion – it was a custom-made coat woven without a seam from top to bottom, too good to be ripped, but good enough to be raffled.

When we come across his cousin in the wilderness, John the Baptist is dressed up in expensive leather clothes, made from the camel and the cattle, just to make a prophetic statement. When Jesus asks his audience about the phenomenal ministry of his cousin John, he also mentions clothes. His parable stories are sometimes clothing sensitive. The forgiving father orders that the best robe to be placed on his prodigal son, and Hither the fatted calf is to be slaughtered, barbecued and served. At the wedding feast the bouncers are ordered to throw the man out who crashes the party without being properly dressed.

He speaks of the rich man, who really has no name, but who is clothed in purple and fine linen and fares sumptuously every day, and that in contrast to the poor man who does have a name – Lazarus – and whose only medical insurance is of the canine variety. In his great Sermon on the Mount, when he is warning us against retaliation and the "tit-for-tat culture" about handing over your shirt along with your jacket! So, clothing gave the Christian message a good start, and made it very fashion conscious.

We also notice how the great missionary preacher, St. Paul, picks up the clothes-conscious theme. We must put on the armor of light by being vigilant Christians. We must put on the breastplate of righteousness. We must put on the Lord Jesus Christ and make no provision for the flesh to fulfill the lusts thereof. In Galatians Chapter 3 there is that powerful Greek word – *endusasthe*- that relates to our baptism. "As many of you as were baptized into Christ have clothed yourselves ("endusasthe") with Christ" (Galatians 3:27 RSV). The writer of the Letter of James warns us against fashion and class prejudice; when the man in fine clothes and gold rings comes into church, we must not give him more honor than the poor man in dirty clothes.

The Early Church Fathers placed great emphasis on the meaning of clothes, as well as on the evils of improperly dressing-up. Cyprian regards the robe of Christ as the sacrament of the unity of the Church. He reminded us that since we are Christ's people cannot be rent. Christ's robe is woven and united throughout; it is not divided by those who possess it. The robe of Christ is undivided, united, connected, and it shows the coherent concord of all of us who put on Christ. This is the way in which declares the unity of the Church.

Chrysostom is very strident as well as eloquent in his homilies on Matthew's Gospel. He preaches that the believer should shine forth by what he has received from God, as well as by what he himself has contributed. He should be discernible by every possible thing, his gait, his look, his garments, and his voice. And here, I cannot resist the temptation of also mentioning two holy grouses on which Chrysostom gets very hot under the collar. First, he warns Christian men against being effeminate looking by wearing sandals woven with ornaments. As far as Chrysostom was concerned, this perverted men to the gestures of women, and caused them by their sandals to grow wanton and delicate.

Secondly, he warned the Christian women against wearing expensive jewelry rather than spending the money on feeding the poor and hungry. He urged women to consider how many hungry bellies they by-passed with this array of ostentation, how many naked bodies they ignored by this satanical display. He suggested that it was better to feed hungry souls than to bore through the lobes of their ears, and to hang from those ears the food of countless poor folk, without purpose or profit. He said that the women should change the ornaments they wore and clothe themselves instead with almsgiving.

So here we are today in the liturgical and ceremonial presence of the successors of Jesus of Nazareth, John the Baptist, Saul of Tarsus, Cyprian, Ambrose, Chrysostom, Augustine, Percival, Donald, and Herman. We are gathered here to ordain and consecrate yet another apostolic leader, and teacher of the Gospel of Jesus Christ. We will not only ordain him; we will also adorn him. Bishops wear attire with strange sounding names – rochet, chimere, pectoral cross, mitre, zuchetto, crozier, mozzetta. Eucharistic vestments worn by bishops and priests have come down to us from Roman secular attire in the second century – the alb was a development from the *tunica,* the chasuble from the *paenula*. The stole was originally worn only by the deacon in the 4th century as a scarf or handkerchief in the Eastern church, and it was known as the *orarium* in the Roman church. The Italians adopted the Gallican word *stola* from the 11th century onwards, from which we derive the English word "stole". The maniple was a development from the *mappula*. The cassock was originally an ankle-length dress in the early Roman Empire. But it is not only the bishops and priests who dress up in church.

One Jamaican clergyman in comparing church-life in the UK with church-life in Jamaica has written these words: "In Jamaica there's more music, contemporary songs, longer sermons, and a greater sense of fellowship. Jamaicans are more expressive, both in the way they talk and the colourful clothes they wear." So, what is this clothing talk all about? You have a right to ask. It all has to do with the New Testament Reading for today from Paul's Letter to the Colossians.

In our reading today, Paul urges us to get dressed. He urges us to put on the right clothes, clothes that have familiar names, clothes that are neither sacred nor secular, but clothes that are heavenly derived and earthly useful. They are the garments of heavenly grace. We must notice something very significant about the clothes we are urged to put on. They are not church clothes. The problem with liturgical attire is that, as pretty and as expensive as they might be, they are only to be worn in church. When the rituals are over the sacred robes are put away. No, Paul is speaking of the clothes for the road, for the streets, the shops, the homes, the trenches, in the struggles for what is right and godly, for the challenging encounters with people anywhere and everywhere. Paul urges us to be dressed up with the virtues and graces of patience, and meekness, and compassion, and kindness, and above all, humility.

These qualities have nothing to do with polyester, or brocade, or cotton, or nylon, or wool, but everything to do with relationships between people and people. There is a culture of Christian clothing that bears the full stamp of moral rectitude, and spiritual integrity, and personal identity. It is an identity of being set apart by God. We are God's chosen ones - both the laity and the non-laity. We have already been spoken for. Jesus reminds us that we have already been chosen. It is an identity of being called out, called together, called upwards to a new and dynamic condition of holiness. What is holiness? Holiness is that location from which we engage the world, rather than the state to which we retreat from it. We are made fully conscious of being loved by God, so much so that God's love radiates through every sinew of our beings, and blossoms forth in transforming and liberating grace, by the way we extend God's gracious invitation to those who hunger and thirst after justice, and peace, and wholeness in life

In our Christian culture, therefore, we dress up to invite others to Christ; we do not dress up to show off. Each of those virtues of which Paul speaks tells its own story of reaching out and touching the other person. "Compassion" is about feeling and suffering with others. "Kindness" makes us wholly available to others. "Humility" ensures that we do not take ourselves too seriously. "Meekness" reminds us of our constant need for God. "Patience" knows how to wait on God, and how to give others the benefit of our doubts for God's sake. These are the garments of Christian grace. We are dressing up to make a difference for the better, not for the worse. Then notice how Paul goes on. He tells us not to leave home without one special piece of garment, for that is the most important of all. It is inherent in our Christian mandate that we affirm and proclaim the supremacy of love; and we can only do this if we are unswervingly committed to the efficacy of faith, and the invincibility of hope. Faith, hope and love are the trinity of Christian virtue. There can be no separation between Christian culture and Christian virtue.

Here in Jamaica, there is as much evidence of a world that is hurting, haunted and hurried, as there is elsewhere in the Caribbean region and beyond. God alone knows how many thousands of Christians throughout the Caribbean offer daily prayer from the depths of their social agony and personal anxiety for peace and stability in the whole world.

Yes, we are living in a hurting, a haunted, and a hurried world – all dressed up in the wrong clothes, and going nowhere on the fast track, just like the bob-sled race. A vicar at a parish church near Rochdale in the Diocese of Manchester in England said earlier this month that young people in the area were always causing him trouble at his church. "Stained-glass windows had been smashed; gangs hung around drinking and smoking drugs in the churchyard; and youths would run in and out of church services taking place in the evening." So, he had to move his services into the Vicarage.

In the country where I now sojourn, we experience the daily horrors of human brutality, the barbaric violation of personal and property rights, child abuse, domestic violence, gang warfare, and high-tech, low-tech, and no-tech crimes. Nowhere is safe, nowhere is pure, nowhere is untouched. But still, everywhere is heavenly, and heaven-loved, for everywhere is a locus and a focus of God's creative and sovereign love, God's liberating power, and God's convulsive Spirit. There is nowhere that cannot be turned upside down, or inside out, and right side up. That is why these words keep ringing in my head: *The Church is there / To cleanse the air.*

Can the air really be cleansed? Are we too late to do anything about it? Can the Church indeed become again a cleansing agent, or does the Church itself need to be cleansed first? Where do we look to find the selfless and sacrificial service, the passion for God's justice, the new paradigms of divine forgiveness, the models of transformative leadership, the courageous risks of genuine faith, or the creative engagement of the manifold gifts of the Spirit in our congregations? Where can we hear a new song that tells again the old, old story of Jesus and His love? What has become of the poor, the maimed, the halt, and the blind, the hungry souls, the thirsty lips, and the imprisoned minds that Jesus claimed as his own kith and kin? Not only did he make the claim with his words, he also made it with his life. He gave his life. He emptied himself. He died. He died on a hill between two thieves, and not on a cross between two candlesticks.

One ancient writer said that as Jesus was lifted up on the cross, he cleansed the air of evil spirits. Those outstretched hands on Calvary made the world clean. Where is the cruciality of the Cross in the life and witness of the church? Although they stripped him of his robes, they could never strip him of his virtue. For it was by that Cross that the powers of the world were exposed as bankrupt – while the power of human virtue and divine grace combined to give the world new life, new air, new hope. Yes, God was in Christ, reconciling the world to himself. He came, he died, he reconciled. He came to start a movement, but he ended up with an institution. How can the church become less of an institution, and begin again to take the movement seriously? Can the church cleanse the air of institutional captivity, and discover again the glorious freedom of the Kingdom of God?

Paul says that we must give it a try. How must we do this? This is where our text for today finally comes into its own. Paul says to the church, to all of us, that what we strive to be on the outside must be resourced, and nurtured, and invigorated, and channeled, by who we are on the inside. In other words, the relational identity that we present to the world on the outside must be rooted and grounded in our spiritual, moral, and doxological character – that is, our praise-worthy and praise-giving character on the inside. We are to allow the Word of Christ to flourish in our innermost beings.

This must surely mean that we sustain an unconditional allegiance to the authority of the Word that is addressed to us by God in so many inspiring ways. By the Word of Christ, we not only listen to Christ, we also speak to Christ, and speak about Christ, and speak in the Name of Christ. We teach and admonish each other for the sake of the movement and not for the lure of dominance or superiority. We exercise godly wisdom as a divine gift and as a shared experience. And we set the highest possible example of gratitude to God in things both small and great. For as the old folks used to remind us: "Ingratitude is worse than witchcraft". And we must not forget to sing, and sing, and sing – for by making a joyful noise to the Lord, we can help to cleanse the air. *The Church is there! To cleanse the air.*

Who will take the lead in this? Whom shall I send, asks the Lord, and who will go for us? Robert Thompson has replied: "Here am I, send me." So here we gather to ordain and consecrate this servant of God for new ministry in the holy Church of God. Here we gather to adorn him with new clothes, all with their symbolic meaning and episcopal splendor. Here we gather to set him apart for new leadership in the church. Here too we gather to renew ourselves, and our own allegiance, to that messianic movement for change and healing, forgiveness and redemption, that Jesus came to build. What shall we say then to Robert himself, as he takes to himself this sacred mantle of mission, this awesome mandate of servanthood, and this prophetic task of apostolic witness? Allow me to speak to him on your behalf.

My Dear Brother in Christ, you may remember that some years ago when you blessed us with your sermon in Washington at the Jamaica Independence Anniversary service, where I was officiating, I made the solemn prediction that one day you would become a bishop. And you may also remember the thunderous applause that this prediction received. Now here we are in this church, witnessing my prediction come to pass. Some may well ask what was the basis for my solemn prediction. I would graciously reply, that in addition to all your priestly qualities and ecclesial qualifications, you stand in line of a special tradition of surnames, since your name ends with the suffix "-son". Jamaican Anglicans seem to like to choose bishops whose names end with "-son". There was Gibson; there was Edmondson; and now there is Thompson.

So, what will Bishop Thompson look like, and sound like, and who will he eventually become? God alone knows; for the future belongs to God. There is one thing that you and I know, however; the God who has called you into this new office will never fail to equip you to make full proof of your ministry. You will surely call to mind quite often the famous prayer of St. Augustine: "Command what you will, and then grant me the means to accomplish it." God always answers such a prayer; and what is more, you can always trust in the trustworthiness of God. For remember, my Brother, God does not call on us to be successful, God only calls on us to be faithful. Whatever you do, however, do not get so busy in serving the Church that you forget to serve your God. You must plant, another will water, and God will always give the increase. What are the seeds and seedlings at your disposal? Let me suggest a few of them – some in Latin, and some in our own language. Some will be related to the episcopal clothes and symbols that you wear.

First let the mitre on your head always remind you that you are to be a ***pastor pastorum***. You are to be a pastor of pastors – leading them into places they have never been before, and even into parts of God's hunting ground that they would rather not go. The mitre must be the sign of the leader for all to see and follow. I often feel that pontifical introit processions are right, but the recessionals are wrong. The bishop should be at the end of the procession into the church but should also be at the head of the procession out of the church. Last in, first out – leading the flock into the world at large. As a pastor of pastors, you must answer the question: "Who ministers to the ministers?" As a pastor of pastors, you must take the lead in energizing your fellow-pastors in the five points of growth in effective ministry, according to Davis. These five growth-points are: *1) Vocational Enlightenment; 2) Holistic Empowerment; 3) Spiritual Enrichment; 4) Ecclesial Endearment; and 5) Radical Engagement.* These five "E's" appear to me to be inherent in the Lord's mandate to us to feed the sheep and tend the lambs.

Secondly, as you wear the ring on your finger, let it remind you of your calling to be a *servus servorum*. You are called to be a servant of servants. Matthew's Gospel tells us that Jesus exercised a threefold ministry of teaching, preaching and healing; but Jesus himself said that he came to serve, not to be served, and to give, and give, and give, his whole life as a ransom for the many. That episcopal ring, Robert, is to be an enduring symbol of being branded and bound as a slave of Christ, and a servant of servants for Christ's sake. As you wear it, however, do not look for any reward or thanks for what you do. Remember Paul's words today that whatever we do in word or deed, we must do everything in the name of the Lord Jesus Christ. Just do the right thing and forget it! Do not wait around for any praise or acknowledgement – for the times are urgent, and the days are evil, and the harvest is even more plenteous today than it was before.

The third Latin seedling has to do with your pectoral cross, regardless of whether you put it in your left shirt-pocket or hang it on your chest. The pectoral cross says: *theologia crucis – theologia gloriae.* That is to say, the only way of glory is the way of the Cross. Yes, Robert, from today onwards you will be placed further on the altar of sacrifice. You will feel again in your body and spirit the crucifying marks of the Lord Jesus Christ. You will encounter disappointments and frustrations, contradictions and controversies, and crises of every variety; nevertheless, that pectoral cross will help you to remember that you should meet every crisis with an open heart, and an open mind, but not always with an open mouth.

The fourth seedling is about the color you will wear. The Latin phrase is one that I am making up especially for you – *agnus Dei – agnus ludorum.* My translation is: "The lamb of God is also the Lamb of the games." The lamb is the sacrificial animal, innocent, defenseless, without blemish, tasty to eat. The lamb's blood is shed; and that blood is more crimson than purple. So, with the episcopal color you wear, try to make it more crimson than purple – for purple was the color that Pontius Pilate wore, while crimson was the color of the blood of Jesus whom he crucified. You will be a lamb of the games that people play in the church. One non-Anglican Jamaican bishop once told me that he was warned at the time of his ordination about three things: he would never be idle; never be hungry; and his clergy would not always tell him the truth. Some of my other bishop-friends have told me that they too have found that to be true; but none of them are here in this service today. So, you will need to be a lamb of God and a lamb of the games people play all at the same time – innocent, strategically dumb, but full of wisdom, full of grace, and full of love.

Here then, are just a few more seeds for planting the trees that will help the church to cleanse the air. **Do not believe your own propaganda**. When they begin to compare you with Freddie, or Harold, or Howard, or Neville, or Willie, your fellow bishops in this place – just clear out as fast as you can. Remember what the Man from Galilee warned us to be careful when people speak well of us. But he also urged us to be happy when we suffer for what is right and just. Again, my Dear Brother, **do not try to make the news – just try your best to make a difference**.

If it be possible, as much as lieth in you, make it a difference for the better and not for the worse.

Further, **pray without ceasing and study without stopping**. A bishop without a steady diet of prayer and a disciplined habit of study is like a singer without a song. How can you sing psalms and hymns and spiritual songs to God without knowing what to sing, or how to sing? I remain convinced that it is through the nurture of the spirit and the mind, by the inner workings of the word of Christ, that our lyrical consciousness can become morally contagious and spiritually inviting. It will enable you to speak truth to power, but it will also guide you to discern the power of truth. Remember, Robert, never try to seek refuge in the comfort of opinion by taking flight from the discomfort of thought.

And one last thing, Robert, never forget those two heavenly words - **THANK YOU**. Paul reminds us of the constant need for gratitude in our hearts. One of the finest letters I have ever received from any bishop came from the late Bishop Swaby. He had to preside at the consecration of two young men – "Dreckie" and "Tony" - as we young clergymen used to call them, at St. Michael's Cathedral in Barbados. I had the honor of assisting him as his chaplain. So, I helped to consecrate those two famous bishops, one of whom is presiding at this service of consecration today! Bishop Swaby wrote me the loveliest letter of thanks in his own hand when he returned to Jamaica. I really do believe that the church can cleanse the air of much ingratitude and thankless-ness when our leaders throughout the whole church, myself included, become more "eucharistic" – more thanks-giving in our living, and not just in our liturgy.

So, may God's Spirit ever encourage and sustain you in your new ministry, my Dear Brother, and may you find much joy and fulfillment as you strive to lead the flock of Christ into pastures green and to waters mild. And may you find daily comfort and strength in the power of God's Holy and Enlivening Spirit.

ANGLICANISM RELOADED II

Port of Spain, Trinidad, February 28, 2016

DO WE SEE JESUS?

My Dear Sisters and Brothers in the Lord, I greet you once again in the Name of Our Lord and Savior Jesus Christ. I am grateful to Bishop Claude for extending this special invitation to me to share in this historic Event. I am nervously conscious of the fact that at your first such Event you welcomed an Archbishop as your Speaker. So, as a retired parish priest, simply leaning on the Lord and my little pension, I would not even dream of trying to match his purple wisdom and heavenly grace. I therefore ask you that you to bear with me for a little while, and also to pray for me that my little efforts may just match the moment if not the Archbishop, especially as my wife and I have come from so far North to be with you today.

I must disclose to you that I have been constantly engaged in the ongoing pilgrimage and struggles of Anglicanism in the Caribbean in some quiet, inconspicuous, and hopefully helpful ways. At least three of the items that you use in your book of worship in CPWI had their origins from my humble domain, including that very long "Form E" in the Prayers of the People. So also was the Caribbean Ecumenical Theme *"The Right Hand of God"*, even though one of my daughters is left-handed! But, thankfully, she has never held that against me! I still serve as Commissary to two Dioceses in the CPWI and consult with other bishops in the Province from time to time.

I come to you, not as a stranger by any means, but as a elder brother and fellow-pilgrim. I come as one who has been sharing in the struggles, the visioning, the challenges, and possibilities, of what it costs, and means, to be Christians in the Caribbean who happen to be Anglicans, but not as Anglicans in the Caribbean who happen to be Christians. It is only when we get our Christian priorities right, and seek first the Kingdom of God, and God's righteousness, that we can truly begin to off-load some of the excess baggage of Anglicanism. We can then re-load with some of the spiritual fuel and cultural fervor that is necessary to follow Jesus at such a time as this. And, guess what, Jesus Christ was neither Christian, nor Anglican!

In the Diocesan material that I have been privileged to review from your Website, and from documents sent to me, I have been able to glean something of the passion and priorities that have been guiding your affairs in this Diocese in recent times. Additionally, as you would have expected, I was able to benefit from several of the insights and visionary ideas from Bishop Claude – one of our conversations lasted for just over 75 minutes! But he never told me what to say! Some of my observations will hopefully reflect the benefits derived from these conversations and reviews, since, as I said to your Bishop, I am coming help you scratch where you say you are itching, rather than to create more itches for you!

Before I forget, however, allow me to make one interesting observation about the pictures of the churches in the four diocesan regions that I saw on your website. As beautiful as the buildings and their surroundings are, I did not see the people, I did not see the altars, nor did I see any signs or images that suggested any congregational activity – either at worship, or work, or witness. We are going explore your preferred definitions of the word "Church" a little later on, but I know for sure that you are all in agreement with St. Paul who told the Athenians that God is not to be identified with human edifices. For better or for worse, your website is your statement in global cyberspace of you claim to be, so whenever you re-load, let us see your faces as well – the bold, bright, and beautiful faces of the followers of Christ in this part of the Lord's Vineyard. Let the whole world see you lifting high the Cross as you "Reclaim, Acclaim, and Proclaim" the Gospel of Jesus Christ, to use your own words. You dare not re-load and then retreat behind the beautiful walls and windows of any edifice.

Your Mission Statement says that you are sent to *"Give honour and glory to God and to work towards helping the people of God to live according to the principles of His Kingdom through participation in the various programme and ministries of the Church"*. As simple and as straightforward as this may sound, it is to be assumed that it emerged out of a prolonged process of discernment and dialogue about what each clause or phrase would mean. I assume for example, that somewhere in that statement the main three-letter word G-O-D stands for a specific way of expressing which God you really mean. People of faith have a way of re-creating God in their own image.

This is what got Mary's boy-child into so much trouble. He was uppity enough to call God "Daddy" – Abba! In our day, God, as you well know, has many names, and many faces, as the current American presidential campaign is telling us loudly and clearly. The American currency carries the motto: "In God We trust"; and some people suggest that the additional words are understood to be: "And In No One Else!" The challenge for us Christians who are trying to identify with Jesus of Nazareth is to "Reclaim" what he said in his own Mission Statement we find in Mark 1:15. Here is what he said: "The time is fulfilled, and the kingdom of God has come near; repent and believe in the good news, the Gospel."

So, in keeping with own Theme for today, let us ask ourselves, "Do We see Jesus in our Mission Statement?" If so, how, and where? Jesus speaks about Repentance – "Metanoia" – Re-loading. Repentance from what, we must ask. Here comes the other three-letter word – S-I-N. It is these two Three-letter words – GOD and SIN – that unconditionally mark out the Mission of Jesus and must drive our sense of mission as well. We are sent into the world by God to name the Sin of the World, to renounce the Sin of the World, and to redeem the World from Sin through the power of grace Divine. There can be no Re-loading of Anglicanism, or any other branch of Christianity, without that genuine and constant Renunciation of Sin – Personal, Structural, Cultural, Systemic, Ecological, or otherwise – and a radical embrace of God's Reconciling and Redemptive Grace. Almost everybody agrees that "Sin is Sweet", the more you practice it the sweeter it seems to get. But guess what – God's Forgiveness and Christ's Redemption is infinitely sweeter!

There is also a Vision Statement for the Diocese and this takes its theme from the Bishop's New Wine Vineyard Program. Now while the Mission Statement speaks of participation in programs, the Vision Statement speaks of transformation of the Diocese as a continuation of a process that has presumably been ongoing. It immediately begs the question of when did that process begin. The Vision Statement of the Diocese of Trinidad and Tobago reads as follows: *To continue the transformation of the Anglican Church in the Diocese of Trinidad and Tobago into a New Wine Vineyard where the entire community of stewards, labourers, tenants and others know and love God and each other, and where all branches are cared for and firmly connected to the vine; and in which the productive processes are high-level, sustainable and accountable functions resulting in a high-quality abundant yield of New Wine.*

Now whereas the membership of the Anglican Church is comprised of laity, deacons, priests, and bishops, this vision designates church membership as stewards, tenants, laborers, and others. We are perhaps left to determine who we would like to be in the Vineyard, and who are the others. And, what about those who are not in the Vineyard at all? Do we have any obligation to reach out for them and bring them in? If that is so, we have not said so. Further, it is not clear who really owns the Vineyard. Neither is it clear who, or what, is the Vine that is mentioned in the Statement. Jesus said that He is the Vine, and we are the branches? Is that what we are saying as well? If that is so why not give His Name honorable mention? Do we see Jesus in our Vision Statement? So, as we engage in some serious re-loading, it seems necessary for these issues to be clarified, so that the image of the Vineyard and the metaphor of high-level and sustainable productivity can be given real body, soul, and spirit. You know, Dear friends, no one really knows how to measure success in the ministry of the Church. This is because it is not determined by buildings, budgets, or bodies; and yet we cannot get by without them.

Besides this, however, the Vision Statement also raises two questions in my mind. The first has to do with the concept of a diocese. I have often cheekily reminded my colleagues that the word "diocese" does not appear anywhere in the Bible, but the word "church" appears very often. The word itself comes from a Greek word that means "house-keeping", or "administration". It first appeared during the time of the Emperor Diocletian in the 4th century when he divided the Roman Empire into twelve administrative regions which he called 'dioceses'. By the 6th century both Eastern and Western bishops patterned their ecclesiastical and temporal authority on the Roman Imperial model, and that has stuck with us ever since.

So, how do we function as collection of congregations grouped together in a single management unit? Are the congregations in service of the diocese, or is the diocese in service of the congregations? It all depends on how the role and function of the bishop is understood by consensus and administered with compassionate love. Bishops have four images to choose from – Chief Steward, Chief Shepherd, Chief Servant or just Chief. As we strive to re-load our Anglican ethos here then, let us be very clear about the dominant image that will be required to hold the administrative unit together and move it forward. I deliberately use the term 'move forward' since we must never remain settled with the grave historical fact that, while Jesus came to inaugurate and establish a Movement, he has in fact ended up with an Institution. The challenge is this: how do we lighten the load of the institution, so that it can travel lightly behind Jesus as the Way, the Truth, and the Life?

The second question is equally important. It has to do with the concept of transformation. Transformation is a radically powerful biblical and theological term, for it is always associated with our understanding of resurrection. Theologians are often careful to declare that resurrection is not resuscitation, as in the case of Lazarus, or the widow of Nain's son. Both died again. Resurrection is not reformation, as in any effort to doing the same old things in some novel way. Resurrection is not even Reincarnation, as we find prominent in some religions. Resurrection is God's transformation, a radical turning of the inside out, a viable snatching of new life out of the jaws of death.

When we Christians are called upon to be risen with Christ and to seek those things that are above, we are being summoned to a life of transformation, radical renewal of mind, heart, and spirit, breaking new ground, and relinquishing as much of the old order that held us socially captive, and spiritually and morally impotent. So, Anglicanism's reloading can find fresh meaning as we seek to practice the art of resurrection, and as we take on board the project of Church transformation.

As we embark on the process of reloading, then, let us be quite clear about what we need to be transformed from, and into what God wills us to be radically transformed.

The Christian Gospel was taken on the road by men and women who made a radically new claim about death and new life. Their claim was that they had seen the Risen Lord. It was a preposterous claim, but they still made it. They took that claim and ran with it in the face of bitter and brutal persecution and death. That's how the saying arose that the blood of the martyrs was the seed of the church. We are a part of their legacy today, a visible and viable part of that growth. Have we seen the Lord? Have we felt his presence in our lives, in our churches, in our communities? How do we see Jesus today? Who is Jesus Christ for us today? How can we liberate the real Jesus from our cultural and historical captivity? Do our religious claims still make sense? If so, what kind of sense, and sense for whom? What difference does our Anglican existence make in the world around us? These are some lingering questions that still need to be asked and answered today.

As we gather today to consider how we are going to re-load and re-charge our Anglican ethos within the framework of the Christian Gospel, and under the guidance of the Spirit of Jesus Christ, what is it about Anglicanism that needs to be re-loaded? History is clear that the Anglican Communion was at one and the same time commensurate with the far reaches of the British Empire. The Church of England was the Mother Church, and all Anglicans throughout the world claimed some form of allegiance to the Archbishop of Canterbury who was appointed by the Queen of England and not chosen by the Communion itself. The Empire is no more. One classical phrase in the history of the English language puts it this way: *"Massa Day Don'!"* A Commonwealth of nations remains, while a Communion of churches is struggling to survive. The Mother Church is now the Grandmother Church, and most recent reports suggest that less than 1 million members attend Anglican churches on any given Sunday in the Church of England. Fame is struggling against Form in Church of England, the seat of Anglicanism itself. What should we re-load? What should we retain? What should we transform? What would we miss?

Theologians often speak of the "Esse", the "Bene Esse", and the "Plene Esse" of the Church. That is, the Essence, the Better Essence, and the Full Essence of what it means to be the Church. How should we translate that from Ecumenical language to Anglican formularies? These are questions to be resolved by the highest councils of the CPWI. One thing is certain, however, and that is that Anglicanism cannot survive as business as usual. One bishop in the Communion has written these words quite recently: "For me, the time has come for the Anglican Communion to go the way of the British Empire."

With that sentiment I entirely disagree, but there is no doubt in my mind that some changes are both necessary and inevitable, and the recent Primates Meeting in England virtually said as much. What the face of Anglicanism will look like in this nation within the next five, ten, fifteen years or so, is for you to determine very shortly – especially the clinical, liturgical, contextual, and ethical aspects of that face. In other words, what exactly will you do to bring about that Anglican face-lift, in your efforts to Re-load Anglicanism in this place?

I suppose it all depends on two major factors that we have inherited from the New Testament itself. One deals with the multiple images of the Church, while the other deals with the twelve tasks of the Church. Let us look at some of those Images.

In the year 1960 the late Dr. Paul S Minear published his classical work entitled *Images of the Church In the New Testament*, and that book was re-published in 2004. In that book he listed some 96 images of the Church, 32 of which he listed as 'Minor images', such as "the salt of the earth", "the vineyard", "the bride of Christ", or "the ambassadors of Christ". He then grouped the other 64 into four other categories: "The People of God" (20); "The New Creation" (16); "The Fellowship in Faith" (17); and "The Body of Christ" (11). It is clear to see from all these metaphors in the New Testament that we are in fact dealing with a Mystical Community, led by the Holy Spirit, which is far more difficult to define and describe tan we can ever imagine or even image adequately.

Things get even more difficult when we affirm our belief in the "communion of saints", which we describe with the words: "part of the host have crossed the flood/ And part are crossing now". We remind ourselves of this not only in the Creed but also in the Sursum Corda. So, as we struggle with how we are to re-load the church in this place, let us make sure that we take into account the most effective and empowering images conceivable and communicable, so that the mission of the Gospel, and the task of meaning-making for all our members, is strengthened by that strong sense of God's call to become who we are already.

In any event, that is what the word "church" means. Karl Barth reminded us that the church is that called community- called out by God, called together by God, and called up by God towards a higher level of meaning and a higher order of witness. This is how we get our three "W's" for the Church – WWW does stand for the World Wide Web, for Christians, however, they stand for "Worship, Work, and Witness". It seems to me therefore, that as you pray earnestly for new directions and fresh ways of following Jesus into the world for which he gave his life, that you will need to embrace images, and groups of images that adequately speak to the realities of our times, never forgetting that Christianity itself is basically an Incarnational religion. It is a religion that takes human flesh very seriously. God became flesh and dwelt among us. This means that we worship a God that has become flesh in the historical person of Jesus Christ, and because of that we dare not demonize the flesh of any living being, nor dare we obscure the face of Christ in the least of us, the lost among us, or the lonely beside us.

Do we see Jesus? Yes, we must, not only in the faces of the vulnerable, the violated, and victimized, but also in the faces of the strong, the sophisticated, and the strangers. So then, if we take hold of the four major Images of Church in the New Testament suggested by Dr. Minear – The People of God, The New Creation, The Fellowship in Faith, and The Body of Christ – and blend them into a rich and powerful mixture of metaphor and meaning, it seems to me that we will be well on our way to some fresh ways of thinking, and radically new ways of reloading the church as a religious organism that is driven by the Spirit, and not as a social organization that is adorned with structural symbolism. Paul reminds that as many as are led by the Spirit of God they are indeed the children of God. Let us urn then to the second New Testament list.

What are the twelve tasks of the Church that we find in the New Testament? This time, I will rely on my own list! Before I do so, however, I would invite you to bring up again the Six Priority Items that the Bishop had promulgated to the Diocese in 2012 in his New Wine Vineyard Document. The priority items were: **Leadership Development, Christian Education, Rationalisation of Resources, Finance, Youth, and Reconciliation.** As I outline the list from the New Testament then, please try to fit those six items into the New Testament framework, for greater theological reinforcement, and deeper biblical enhancement.

Task Number One: TEACHING – This is one of the three dimensions of the ministry of Jesus that is mentioned in Matthew 9:35. The Church is a Didactic Movement, teaching not just the Christian Faith tradition, but also about the ways of the world, and how to navigate through all the changes and challenges faced by the Christian.

Task Number Two: PREACHING – This is the second dimension of the ministry of Jesus. The Church is entrusted with the message of the Gospel, the Good News, and it is thus a Kerygmatic Community. It preaches the Gospel in such a way that men and women are invited to hear, accept, respond, and repent. The whole story of the Acts of the Apostles is the story of the movement of the Kerygma from Jerusalem to Rome. The Gospel is comprised of the Five "F's" – Forgiveness, Feeding, Friendship, Freedom, and the Future.

Task Number Three: HEALING – Not only was the ministry of Jesus characterized by his healing activities, but the Early Church established itself as a Therapeutic Community. This task is critically important in the life of the Church in every age, since the sin of the world, and the sickness in the world, are diametrically opposed to the saving work and will of God in Jesus Christ. We are to remember that Jesus came into the world that all may have life and have it in all its fullness. Every congregation must be seen and known to be a therapeutic fellowship, rather than a collective source of disease and decay, whether physical, spiritual, or ethical. Church people must never become the butt of sick jokes, or the focus of social scorn and constant derision. We are called to be a critical part of the cure, not a chronic mode of the disease.

Task Number Four: WORSHIP – This is the most obvious and conspicuous sign of the Church's function and existence. The liturgical life of the church absorbs most of its time, talents and resources. The worshipping church gives form and expression to the faith which it professes, makes meaning possible to its membership, and corporately practices the art and ritual of the presence of God, not only within its walls, but more particularly in the world to which it is sent by God. Let us never forget that the Greek word "Leitourgeia", from which the English word "Liturgy" is derived, was originally a description of what happens in the marketplace and not in the shrines. So, Liturgy moved from the world into the church; and it is time for it to move back into the world with sacred meaning and missionary zeal.

Task Number Five: FELLOWSHIP – This task is of central importance in the life of the Church. Of course, the supreme act of fellowship is the sacred meal that sacramental links us in mystical fellowship with Christ himself. The essence of fellowship is the ethic of sharing, and this is most powerfully demonstrated not only in the feeding miracles in the Gospels, but also in the inaugural culture of the Apostolic church where the principle of common goods and common needs was implemented in a collective process called "Koinonia". This is a principle that not only signifies mutual participation, but also mutual caring and responsibility. We are to bear one another's burdens, and so fulfill the law of Christ.

Task Number Six: SERVICE – This task places the church squarely in the continuation of the ministry of Jesus himself. He saw himself as a servant – "The Son of Man came not to be served, but to serve, and to give his life as a ransom for many." (Mark 10:45 RSV). In my book entitled *Serving With Power*, I draw attention to as many as eight different words that are used for "servanthood" and "serving" in the New Testament. The serving church is that which most authentically seeks to embody the mission and ministry of Christ. Do we see Jesus in our midst? That is one area where we should look for him. Do we always see him at work among us? Quite often, I find that congregations need to eliminate their collective "serve-us" mentality and embrace a strong determination to practice the ministry of "service" for Christ's sake.

Task Number Seven: STEWARDSHIP – Every Christian is called to be a steward, a trustee, a keeper and a dispenser of the manifold gifts and mysteries of God's providential and creative love. It is true that the promotion of stewardship is often linked with the T-T&T syndrome. That does not stand for the Trinidad and Tobago syndrome, but rather for the Time, Talents and Treasure accountability that applies to each of us. Christian Stewardship extends far beyond those three "T's", however, and it also includes the three "V's" – Value, Virtue, and Vigor. Clearly, one of the Bishop's Six Priority Items – Rationalisation of Resources, falls neatly within this task, if it begins with each faithful member and radiates outwards and upwards, rather than making the corporation that center of impulsion.

Task Number Eight: EDIFICATION – The letter to the Ephesians challenges us very strongly about the nature of the church as God's household, God's family, God's building. It is necessary for each one to see him/herself as a builder. This also is strongly encouraged by Paul in his Corinthian correspondence. Whatever we do for God and his church must be edifying, constructing, and shoring up the nature of the spiritual community. This is extremely relevant to what we are about today in our efforts to re-load, re-charge, and reinforce the mission and ministry of the church in this place. Every word, every measure, every program, every sermon, every service, must be evaluated in terms of its edifying potential. If it does not fit, then we must quit!!

Task Number Nine: WITNESSING – You shall be my witnesses, says Jesus, whether it is in Jerusalem, Antioch, Moscow, Port-of-Spain, or Scarborough. The kind of witness that Jesus envisages and enjoins carries with it some very costly factors, including the possibility of martyrdom. That is why the word for "witness" and the word for "martyr" come from the same root. Witnessing involves costly discipleship, that is, taking up the cross (not only in a liturgical procession!) in one's life, and following daily with the power of truth along the way of Crucifixion, Confrontation, Contradiction, Conviction, and Conversion. Unless we are prepared to face up to the possibility of these five "C's" in our experiences, whether seasonally, or steadily, it might be better just to pack up, turn back, and look for some easier roads in life. The practice of genuine Christianity is just not easy at all, at all, at all! There is no such thing as cheap grace for living this life, even if we now enjoy cheap gas for driving around in our cars and SUV's.

Oddly enough, I happen to believe that the witnessing church will sometimes do better in shunning processions and public displays of piety and embracing the quiet and incisive ways of making a sustainable difference for the better in people's lives. Let me hasten to assert, however, that this is by no means a criticism of Anglicanism Re-loaded II, which has taken five years to happen again. It is merely pointing to the question of what will happen between Re-Loaded II and Re-loaded III. After all, God made us one at a time, why can't we try to bear witness to others one at a time? I can still hear William Shakespeare warning us that "Small showers last long, but sudden storms are short"!

Task Number Ten: RECONCILIATION – This starts at the very heart of the work of Christ, the saving will of God, and the vision of the Kingdom of God. The central message of the New Testament is found in II Corinthians 5:19 (RSV)– *"In Christ, God was reconciling the world to himself, not counting their trespasses against them, and entrusting to us the message of reconciliation."* The brokenness in the creation is confronted by the re-creative and liberating work of God in Christ, so that the followers of Jesus no longer have to live between the cracks in creation, nor should they accept all the brokenness in life as the final order of their world. The Gospel says that it is not true that although all the king's horses, and all the king's men could not put Humpty Dumpty together again, that God cannot bring about what I call the *DE-HUMPTI-DUMPTI-FICATION* of the world. Reconciliation begins with each of us as individual members of the Body of Christ, and issues forth through all the many phases of the religious community, the national community, and the global community.

Task Number Eleven: - LIBERATION – The Gospel of Jesus Christ is the Gospel of Freedom. The message of the Gospel is carried forward with that unconditional trust in that unconditionally free God. To listen to St. Paul again, he writes in Galatians 5:1 (RSV) *"For freedom, Christ has set us free, stand fast therefore, and do not submit again to a yoke of slavery"*. The most challenging question for modern day Christians is not so much what they want to be free from, nut what they work to be free for. Without a doubt, modern forms of slavery still abound, especially within the world of social media and its multiple machines.

But the church is essentially the celebrative community of God's freedom, so that any form of enslavement, any form of dehumanization, any form of subjugation, must surely constitute the crucifixion of Christ all over again. We need to remain conscious of what Jesus Christ has saved us from, while at the same time using our freedom as a spiritual and moral instrument for setting others free. Liberation, Emancipation, Transformation, Redemption, call it whatever you will, if it re-presents to the world that central fact of God's saving will made plain in Christ's work of salvation. After all, Do we see Jesus? Yes, we do! His very Name means – God Saves!

Task Number Twelve: - COMPASSION – The Church of God is called into being to embody and demonstrate the Compassionate Love of God through Jesus Christ. This is the central meaning of John 3:16-17 (RSV) – *"For God so loved the world that he gave his only Son, that whoever believed in him should not perish but have eternal life. For God sent the Son into the world, not to condemn the world, but that the world might be saved through him."* The Church is called to be that Compassionate Community in every respect, because it is driven and sustained by the supreme virtue of Love. Love happens to be the only word that functions as a synonym for God. Love is God, and God is Love, and Compassion is radiated through the Church by virtue of the Spirit who guides the Church. We sing of the Spirit in that well-known hymn: *As Thou in bond of Love dost join / The Father and the Son / So fill our hearts with mutual love, / And knit our hearts in one.* (Hymns Ancient & Modern, #208, verse 2)

These then are the twelve tasks of the Church that I find in the New Testament. They provide a very important matrix, or template, or checklist, or guidebook, for engaging in any re-loading of the church, whether it is Anglicanism, Catholicism, Pentecostalism, or Orthodoxy. I have no doubt that in the time to come you will be able to locate your Six Priority Items in one or more of these New Testament tasks. In the meantime, however, allow me to suggest another Six Secondary Items for your consideration. These would be focused more on congregational life and vitality, and not so much on the higher workings of the Church at the Diocesan level. These are more for the laborers and tenants in the trenches and the vignettes in the New Wine Vineyard. It might also be considered that these secondary items might be subsumed in the broader explanations of the Six Priority Items.

My suggested list is as follows: **Partnership-in-Mission, Spiritual In-Reach, Anglican Outreach, Health & Wellness Ministry, Techie-Evangelism, and Social Ecumenism**. It is quite possible that with a substantial amount of congregational dialogue, and collegial discernment amongst the clergy, that a powerful surge of Missional Engagement, Transformational Leadership, and Spiritual Enrichment, can continue to move this diocese forward into places and circumstances that you would rather not go. That is the crazy thing about serving God. The crazy thing about serving God, either personally, or corporately, is that God's sense of humor is so outlandish, so mysterious, so convulsive, that we are driven by God's Grace to make the impossible possible, and the rough ways of life navigable, exciting, and wonderful.

Finally, we return to our theme for today: "**Do we see Jesus?**" Can we see Jesus? Or is it that we would prefer to recreate Jesus in our own convenient images? If you really want to see Jesus just look for the "Fish". That was how the early Christians symbolize Him. The Greek word for "Fish" is **ICHTHUS**. It gave them an Acrostic that stood for "Jesus-Christ-Son-of-God-Savior". Whatever you choose, just do something to find Jesus in your own life. So, let me leave you with yet another Acrostic that also spells out the Name of Jesus. If the earlier

Acrostic focused on our inner life, with all the spirituality that God makes available to us, this second Acrostic offers a way of looking for **JESUS** in the world around us. Here we go: **J – for JUSTICE; E – for EMPOWERMENT; S – for SERVICE; U – for UPLIFTMENT; S – for SOLIDARITY.** This final S stands for "Solidarity", not so much with the rich and the powerful, but more so with the poor, the oppressed, the marginalized, and the abandoned among us. If we are really trying to find Jesus in our midst, listen to where he says we must look for him, that is amongst the least and the lost.

Brothers and Sisters in The Lord, that sounds good enough for me. I trust that it is good enough for you as well. May God richly bless us all. AMEN.

Sermon at St. Michael's Cathedral, Barbados

At The Inauguration of the St. Michael's
Centre for Faith & Action

Feast of Pentecost, June 4th, 2017

But the Counselor, the Holy Spirit, whom the Father
will send in my name, he will teach you all things,
and bring to your remembrance all that I have said
to you. (John 14:26 RSV)

My Dear Friends, here we are today, celebrating the Feast of Pentecost. This is a major festival of the Church for many reasons. Pentecost brings to a close the formal celebration of the Easter season, while at the same time it reinforces the fact that it is in the Christian's DNA to practice the faith and the art of resurrection every moment of every day. We practice the art of resurrection every time we snatch the sinews of life out of the jaws of death, or when we strike one for Jesus against all the death-making and dehumanizing forces and attitudes in our social culture and human relationships.

Pentecost signals the re-birth of the Church as the Pilgrim People of God, moving forward with a Mission. It is the Mission of the Gospel of Jesus Christ, and it is still committed to ushering in the Kingdom of God as a Movement of the Spirit, and not as an Institution of our social structures. It has often been noted that Jesus came to inaugurate a Movement, but he has ended up with an Institution. Pentecost brings new life to the Trinitarian understanding of who God is, how God works, and why God calls. I am sure that you will already have noticed the Trinitarian framework in our text – the Father, as God for us, Jesus, as God with us, and the Spirit, as God within us.

Pentecost enables us to feel within ourselves, and amongst ourselves, not only the manifold gifts of the Spirit, but more especially the manifold workings of the Spirit. The Spirit of God creates, often bringing something out of nothing. The Spirit of God empowers, often making God's strength more perfect in our weakness. The Spirit of God collaborates, often building unity out of division, and community out of diversity. The Spirit of God convulses, often turning things upside down, often bringing divine chaos out of human order, disrupting the status quo and generating such surprises that we often call mysteries or even miracles. This is what we just sang in the Magnificat; God puts down the high and the mighty, and exalts those of low degree, or no degree. Never forget that the Song of Mary in Luke's Gospel is followed up by her own boy child's embrace of Isaiah's Song in Chapter 61 when he goes back to his home cathedral in Nazareth. *"The Spirit of the Lord God is upon me, because the Lord has anointed me to bring good tidings to the afflicted; he has sent me to bind up the brokenhearted, to proclaim liberty to the captives, and the opening of the prison to those who are bound; to proclaim the year of the Lord's favor, and the day of vengeance of our God."* (Isaiah 61:1,2 (RSV)

The Spirit of God communicates, often disclosing the Truth, often enlightening the Ignorant, and often teaching the Faith. This is precisely what Jesus is promising in our text for today; the Spirit is to be the *PARAKLETOS,* the Advocate, the Advocate of God, the Advocate for the Gospel, the Teacher of the Faith of Jesus Christ. He will teach you everything, says Jesus, and will remind you gradually, remind you privately, remind you constantly, of the whole message and meaning of what it means to follow Jesus. The Christian learns by being reminded gradually and reminded often of the need to follow Jesus. It has been rightly said that the Christian who seems to feel that he or she has nothing more to learn is the Christian who has not even begun to understand what is really meant by the doctrine of the Holy Spirit.

So, my Dear Friends, I would make bold to believe and to assert that the Vestry and authorities of St. Michael's Cathedral have been led by the Spirit of God to be imaginatively creative, to be courageously convulsive, to be strategically empowering, to be selflessly collaborative, and to be faithfully communicative. Of course, although the Cathedral is named after a mythical figure and his mythical companions, the very meaning of the name "Michael" – "who is like God?" links the Cathedral itself with the very nature of the Holy Spirit. To speak of the

Spirit of God is always to refer not only to the nearness and presence of God, but also to the leading and guiding force of that very God. Let us be fully persuaded that what is being launched today is yet another venture of this historic establishment that is divinely inspired, prayerfully conceived, and corporately embraced. Why these sentiments are significant is the fact that not all ventures launched by this, or any other congregation, ever reach a sustained cruising altitude.

What comes to mind is the 1875 initiative to convert St. Michael's Cathedral into a concert hall. This was the pet project started by Bishop John Mitchinson. On New Year's Day the year before, he had preached at St. Matthew's church about the beauty of the old Temple of Jerusalem, its noble and antiquarian architecture. He suggested that the beauty of Church architecture was useful to excite the admiration of the sense, and more so "to appeal to the higher and nobler instincts of our nature, with a view to encourage a more liberal dedication of our worldly substance to the service of the Most High." Mitchinson expressed the view that the absence of beauty in church buildings in Barbados was due to what he called a "niggardly regard to save money." So, he put the idea to the St. Michael's Vestry, which formed a Special Committee to investigate the matter, led by the Bishop himself. By September of 1875 the Vestry endorsed the idea of erecting a new cathedral that would be "more conformable to the antiquity of the Diocese and the importance of the colony."

Bishop Mitchinson had launched an appeal fund with a pledge of 1000 pounds over five years. The famous Rector of St. Michaels' The Rev. Thomas Clarke pledged 50 pounds over the same period, perhaps indicating his very faint support for the project. By the end of March of that year the New Cathedral Committee announced that they had received just over 5000 pounds in pledges, and that the new project would begin when they had accumulated 10,000 pounds. The idea created quite a stir in Barbados, especially as a result of the exchange of correspondence between Bishop Mitchinson and the famous planter Sir Graham Briggs. Briggs thought that there was far too much poverty in Barbados at the time for the church to be planning to build a new cathedral.

Well, as you all know, the Confederation riots erupted the following year. The Bishop somehow grew increasingly unpopular as time went by; and he left Barbados in 1881, and the new cathedral project was abandoned. In spite of the otherwise good work that he had done during his brief episcopate, especially in the field of Education, and launching the forerunner to the Barbados Scholarship to Oxford and Cambridge, he felt that his ministry here had been a failure. As he departed, the Bishop claimed that was very unpopular indeed during his stay in Barbados, to the point where he thought that his episcopate was a failure. Those feelings of the Bishop surely raise a question for all of us who are called into the ordained ministry of the church, anywhere and anytime. What are we to measure in the ministry, either in terms of success, or failure? I have always been taught that God does not call on us to be successful, God only calls on us to be faithful.

Today, the St. Michael's Cathedral story continues, and this time there are no sorry situations to report, as far as I am aware. We are about to launch the **St. Michael's Centre for Faith and Action.** The mission of the Centre, it is said, "will be to engage the nation on issues of public interest with an emphasis on the integration of Faith and Action."

My assumption is that the Church in this place is already engaging itself on such issues, since it is impossible to be an authentic agent of change without first becoming a changed agent. The message of Jesus is as clear as clear can be in the Sermon on the Mount, we dare not challenge others unless we have first challenged ourselves. The main ongoing challenge for all of us as modern-day Christians is to create a very forceful, faithful, and fertile integrative encounter between what we call Orthodoxy and Orthopraxis. Orthodoxy means right belief, while Orthopraxis means right conduct, right behavior, and right witness. In popular parlance we are called by Jesus to "walk the talk" rather than "talk the walk".

The Motto for the proposed Centre is: *"Pursuing Knowledge, Justice and Kindness"*. This invokes a very noble and yet complex task, especially since Justice and Kindness are virtues in themselves, while Knowledge is not. Furthermore, we are now globally immersed in a virtual information jungle; some would prefer to call it an ocean. Whatever the metaphor we choose, the fact is that the pursuit of Truth in this day and age of what has become known as "alternative facts", or "fake news", is far from being identical with the pursuit of true knowledge, apart from knowing that "fake news" is fake. Local Barbadian political discourse has sometimes made a distinction between truth and impressions. It is the pursuit of Truth that will be characteristic of the Pentecostal genesis of this Centre, and this will become so pivotal to the Centre's moral worth and national effectiveness. The promise of the Holy Spirit to teach the Faith is also linked with the promise of the Holy Spirit to guide us into all Truth, chiefly because the Holy Spirit is indeed the Spirit of Truth.

The faith of the Church is rooted and grounded in the sacred imagination of its members, in the faithful proclamation of its message, and the progressive engagement of its mission. This is the mystical connection between Word and Sacrament, and this is essence of the word "remembrance" (*anamnesis*), which Jesus uses for both halves of our Christian life. Through Word and Sacrament Faith and Action vigorously combine to discern a deeper knowledge of the Truth, guided by the Spirit of God who is the source of all Truth. Perhaps it will not be too bold for me to assume therefore, that the Motto of the Centre will also be the Mantra for the Centre, and that the Mantra will generate and sustain a relentless search for Knowledge. I am speaking about a deep and persistent struggle to wrestle with knowledge of the Truth – that is, the truth about God, about God's world, about God's Church, and about God's work in bringing divine chaos out of human order.

Allow me to say a little more about this last assertion. There can hardly be any doubt in anyone's mind that we are have been living not merely in a post-modern era, but also in a post-Christian age. Ideas about "God" have multiplied exponentially. Traditional religious beliefs and practices have been experiencing increased competition for any number of reasons. Countless people within and beyond the church have tended to thrive by re-imagining, or else re-creating "God" in their own image, with all the cultural and ideological captivity that is inherent in such attitudes. Atheism and Agnosticism have been gaining traction amongst the millennials and the technologically oriented generations right across the age spectrum. More and more of our young and not-so-young now prefer to claim that they are SBNR's (Spiritual But Not Religious), having little or nothing more to do with organized religion. Sources of moral authority in modern societies are no longer easy to define, let alone identify.

What it means to be human is no longer a commonly held approach to life, given all the surges of materialism, individualism, terrorism, excessive pragmatism, and rugged globalism. These are the realities that we face today. This is the theatre of the battle that is being waged between the Common Faith of the Gospel of Jesus Christ, and the Action of the Gospel of Common Sense. So, shall we fight the Good Fight of Faith? And how shall the work and witness of the **St. Michael's Centre For Faith and Action** put Faith to work in Barbados, and hopefully beyond? Someone has rightfully said that the "Faith that works is the Faith that works."

Apart from its proposed Motto, the Centre will set five goals for its work. These are: (1) To engage with questions of faith and action. (2) To function as a community of moral deliberation. (3) To create an environment that is conducive for dialogue and partnerships. (4) To cultivate and facilitate an atmosphere for research and publication, especially in public theology. (5) To respond to social needs, especially to the vulnerable and the marginalized. Although the word "Justice" it is not mentioned explicitly in these five goals, the struggle and advocacy for social equity and transformative justice will undoubtedly inform and drive most of what the Centre hopes to accomplish. The focus on public theology will derive its energy from the vibrant reflection on practical theology, while the sources of practical theology will be inspired an enlightened by a careful and prayerful re-reading of Sacred Scripture.

If this is to be the case, let us explore in conclusion some of the signposts that the pilgrimage of Faith will bring the Centre into a fertile response for Biblical Action. Let us see what the Holy Spirit as the Great Teacher of Truth will bring to our minds now. Faith will demand Action with respect to Human Rights and people's rights to be fully human Faith demands Action with respect to Redistribution of Resources and opportunity. Faith demands Action with respect to Racism and Racial Injustice here and elsewhere. The fate of Simon of

Cyrene who was forced to bear another man's burden comes to mind, even if it was to help that innocent Nazarene who was struggling with his piece of the Cross up the hill of Golgotha. Simon was a Black man. Faith demands Action with respect to human Relationships, especially with those who may be different from ourselves. The story of the Good Samaritan comes to mind. Faith demands Action with respect to Reconciliation of all shapes and forms of social forces and human classes. We live in a broken world. God demands that Christian Faith and Action converge, conspire, and confront all forms of brokenness, wherever they happen to exist.

So, My Dear Friends, let us congratulate and commend the Dean and his colleagues for this very timely and progressive initiative in establishing the **St. Michael's Centre For Faith And Action**. I look forward to hearing great things about its work and effectiveness. I will also look forward to sharing in perhaps just a little piece of the Action in my capacity as a proud citizen of Barbados. The virtual connectivity and the cyber culture will help to make such involvement feasible and practicable. I trust that the Centre will become virtual space for Ecumenical fervor, prophetic advocacy, and spiritual enrichment. And above all, may the Holy Spirit so guide and empower all who share in the style and substance of its work, so that we may all come to know Jesus more clearly, and follow Jesus more clearly, as we strive to love one another more dearly. To God be the Glory, both now and evermore. AMEN.

NECA AT ONE SEVENTY-FIVE: TO THRIVE, TO THRIVE, OR JUST SURVIVE?

A Lecture to Celebrate the 175th Anniversary of the Diocese of North Eastern Caribbean and Aruba St. John's, Antigua May 24th, 2017

My Dear Sisters and Brothers in the Lord, I am truly grateful to the Bishop of this Diocese, and the Planning Committee for this year-long celebration, for inviting me to deliver these two lectures, both here and in St. Kitts. I want you to know that I consider it a great privilege and honor to have been so invited; and I trust that my reflections with you will in some way help to make even a little difference for the better in the life, the culture, and the mission, of this Diocese as a whole. This is the Diocese that has reared me, called me, trained me, supported me, and sent me forth to train others for ministry. I have tried my best to honor and cherish the great responsibilities that such investments have demanded, and I have zealously tried to burn no bridges behind me, nor to miss any available opportunities to further the work and mission of the Church in these parts.

A famous man once said that a "prophet is not without honor except in his own country and among his own people." While I have always tried to keep that saying prominent in my mind, I have endeavored neither to function nor dress like a prophet, since prophets are usually stoned by their own people. Neither have I attempted to embrace that triple office of prophet-priest-and-king with which that man was designated by the three wise men in the story in Matthew's Gospel.

I was made a Deacon in St. John's Cathedral on December 21st, 1965, St. Thomas's Day, and ordained a Priest in St. George's Church, Basseterre, on August 6th, 1966, the Feast of the Transfiguration. Both ordinations were presided over by my life-long pastor, mentor, and Father-in-God, Bishop Donald Rowland Knowles of blessed memory. His model of ministry was the other triple function of Jesus, as

Teacher-Preacher-Healer which we also find in the Gospels. That is the model of ministry that I have tried to embody and embrace throughout my fifty-two years of ordained ministry. That is also the basis on which I have chosen to share these reflections with you in this lecture.

The Church has been called to be a Didactic community through its teaching; to be a Kerygmatic community through its preaching; and to be a Therapeutic community through its healing properties, and by its hurting propensities. The mission of the Church is to help its people to thrive, and to thrive progressively and counter-culturally, especially in the face of a climate and culture in which they are merely struggling to survive. Accordingly, I have entitled this lecture, NECA AT ONE SEVENTY-FIVE: TO THRIVE, TO THRIVE, OR JUST SURVIVE? So, let us begin.

Let me call to mind the folk-memory of a man who was one of the most important and significant Anglicans in Antigua during the last century. He performed a most important function in the worship and culture at the center of local Anglicanism. He was an Antiguan who knew who he was, who affirmed his own dignity and identity, and who unwittingly embodied both the contrasts and the continuities inherent in the history of the Diocese of Antigua. He worked at the St. John's Cathedral, which was not only the tallest building on the Island at that time, but which also represented that towering edifice and symbol of the presence of "Big Church" in the society.

I never knew his real name, but that did not matter. Antiguans have traditionally been more familiar with people's nicknames than they are with their official names – for generally, nicknames were not always badges of derision. They were more closely embraced as badges of narrative identity, or terms of social familiarity and cultural endearment. A good example of our local cultural heritage was prominently aired within this past year when a famous newspaper seller at the Airport was called home to rest. But neither the church community, nor the radio stations, could bring themselves to announce his popular nickname in public, although all of us knew who had died. Other Antiguan nicknames have been less uncomfortable - such as "Juicyman", "Grey-ghost", "Dead-an'-Live", "Spoon", "Dribbler", or "Bang-kiddy". However, the famous Anglican to whom I earlier referred was known as "Pick-up Jimmy". I learned a lot about Pickup Jimmy from my mother, Edna Clarke, who was, for me at least, another very important Anglican in this country.

Pick-up Jimmy was a full Antiguan man, black, black, black, who knew who he was. But Pick-up Jimmy was also a local Anglican metaphor. He belonged to the Anglican Church, and he worked in it and for it, but the Anglican Church did not belong to him. The Anglican Cathedral had been employing Black people for various functions. There is a record of the death of one Mr. Samuel Jones on February 9th, 1889, who had been born a slave, and who had served as Sexton of the St. John's Cathedral for quite some time. With respect to Pick-up Jimmy, however, the story is told that there was an organ recital planned for the St. John's Cathedral one night early in the twentieth century.

All the attendees were well dressed, fully assembled, and waiting eagerly for the recital to begin. Pick-up Jimmy was to blow the bellows of the great cathedral organ, and a famous local organist was to perform. As the appointed hour arrived and the recital was to begin, Pick-up Jimmy was leaning over the balcony rail looking down at the audience below, while the organist was bewildered that there was no wind in the bellows. Pick-up Jimmy was not at his post to pump. So, when the organist asked him why he was not pumping the bellows, Pick-up Jimmy promptly replied: "You play, you play! These people didn't come to hear me pump, they only came to hear you play, so play on!"

In my mind, this story has survived in the local Anglican narrative folklore as a signal of the Classism, Racism, Cultural Alienation, Social Accommodation, and Religious Transplantation that have riddled the history of Anglicanism in the Caribbean as a whole. I have often maintained that the movement of European invaders to the so-called New World was not simply driven by the exploits and adventures of Christopher Columbus, who in 1492 sailed the ocean blue. Columbus happened to come upon lands by a navigational mistake and met up with peoples who had never invited him, and about whom he knew nothing. Those who followed in his wake were driven by four very powerful factors: Greed, Gold, Glory, and God.

So strategically interwoven were these four forces, that the European invaders came to believe that what they had found, conquered, and exploited were all given to them by God. Not only did the Caribbean become the new expansion of European economic, military, and social exploits, it also became the new incubator for global racism. Accordingly, in addition to the four "G's" that I have just mentioned – Greed, Gold, Glory, and God, the European exploiters established in the region plantations and colonies that were driven by the force of four "S's" – Slavery, Sugar, Superiority, and Subjugation.

These four forces were critical for them in their quest to maintain power, dominance, and social control, while advancing their own industrial and economic designs. Sugar was the King. Plantation establishments were the order of the day. Every form of existence had to subsist and survive under the cruel shades and stormy shadows of the plantation. The perennial challenge of Caribbean history has always been to find a satisfying answer to the question: How do you turn plantations into societies, without moving from one form of plantation dominance to the subjugation of another form of plantation whether it is hotel, government, political or industrial establishment? This was where the function of religion came into the picture, with its priests and prayer-books, and riddled with all forms of political control and social contradictions. In the British Caribbean for sure, the churches emerged out of the plantations and the plantation mentality, so much so that the Church of England in British colonies was essentially the collective and consummate chaplaincy and protector of the plantation system.

On June 5th 1932, there was a special service of thanksgiving in St. John's Cathedral to celebrate the three hundredth anniversary of British colonization in these parts. The Anglican Church in these regions emerged, and was sustained for centuries, as extensions of the plantations. Slavery, Sugar, Superiority, and Subjugation rigidly combined to maintain a form of organized religion. This ensured that the plantation system produced what was expected of it for all sectors of the societies, and for the furtherance of the means of production to be blessings from the God of the planters. That underscored the origins and survival of harvest festivals among the churches.

This was the historical context into which the Anglican Church was rooted and grounded. This was the dominant culture that established various forms of colonial control and social stratifications. This too was the climate in which the Diocese of Barbados was formed by the British Government to incorporate the Leeward and Windward Islands, and Trinidad, Tobago, and British Guiana in 1824. This was the expansion and re-configuration of the cause for which the Diocese of Antigua was established in 1842. Some congregations that had been established since the 17th century, under the supervision of the Bishop of London at first, and then under the supervision of the Bishop of Barbados, were now grouped together into one Diocese, with a diversity of island cultures and plantation governance, but driven mainly by geographical convenience.

Bishop John Mitchinson, the Coadjutor Bishop at the time, described the Diocese in 1882, some 40 years later. He said that the Diocese was comprised of fourteen islands that were not bound by any ties of national identity and separated by a large spread of sea. This meant that there were obvious tendencies towards some disintegration, accompanied by insularity and some modes of 'Congregationalism'.

Thus, these islands, like birds of a feather, were forged together. So, 1842 marked the beginning of a new ecclesiastical experiment in cultural and colonial diversity, as newly freed slaves were now harnessed in religious cleavage with their former owners under the leadership of their own Bishop. A Diocese emerged, a Bishop was enthroned, but the Church still maintained its business as usual with conditions of race, class, power, and status determining within itself its own rigid distinctions. These were distinctions between the high and the low, the rich and the poor, blacks and Whites, masters and servants, citizens and subjects, lettered and unlettered, those who were in, and those who were out, and those who were neither in nor out.

One hundred and seventy-five years ago this year, this Diocese was formed, not so much to challenge, confront, or change the climate, culture, or the context of the day. It was not formed to transform the realities of unwholesome and oppressive conditions, such as they were for the masses of the people in these islands. The Diocese was formed to make a good system work better for those who benefitted from it, while they made sure that the ex-slaves who had just been emancipated some eight years earlier, in 1834, would keep themselves beholden to planters, priests, and pirates, for their very survival.

But where did the very concept of a "diocese" come from in the first place? There were churches, and churches, and churches, and groups of organized faith-communities that held to some common forms of worship, ritual, customs, and conduct. I have often cheekily reminded my colleagues that the word "diocese" does not appear anywhere in the Bible, but the word "church" appears very often. The word "diocese" itself comes from a Greek word that means "house-keeping", or "administration". It first appeared during the time of the Emperor Diocletian in the 4th century, when he divided the Roman Empire into twelve administrative regions which he called 'dioceses'. By the 6th century both Eastern and Western bishops patterned their ecclesiastical and temporal authority on the Roman Imperial model, and that has stuck with us ever since, and bishops have identified themselves by wearing the imperial color of purple, or crimson, and are still addressed as "Lordships".

How do we function as a collection of congregations grouped together in a single management unit? Are the congregations in service of the diocese, or is the diocese in service of the congregations? It all depends on how the role and function of the bishop, as the leader and overseer, is understood by consensus, and administered with pastoral competence and compassionate efficiency. Universally, bishops have tended to choose from one of seven images by which to conduct themselves, and to assume the mantle of leadership in their dioceses. These images I would list as the following: Pastor of Pastors, Chief Steward, Chief Shepherd, Chief Servant, Chief Executive, Commander-in-Chief, or just Chief. It would make for a very interesting historical study for someone else to review the range of episcopates over these past 175 years in this diocese, and to assess which image most aptly applied to the type of leadership and quality of ministry of each bishop so far. We shall return to "bishops" later.

The official Theme for this 175th anniversary celebration is: ***Celebrating Our Heritage; Seizing The Moment: Embracing The Future***. I would hasten to enquire about the nature of the heritage that we are to celebrate, and this for three very significant reasons. First, the history of Anglicanism in the region in general, and in these islands in particular, has been a very mixed bag of circumstances and memories, mainly as a continuation of the conditions and realities which I have already been describing about its origins in these parts. Secondly, the experiences of congregations in these islands, and between islands, have varied so much that the identification of common sources of pride and praise, of priorities and progress, would be difficult to accomplish. One island's story, like the stars, differs from another island's story in glory.

Thirdly, the evolution of the Anglican Church from being a missionary, social, and religious enterprise into becoming a genuine community of faith, witness, and service, has been both challenging and paradoxical. The challenge has mainly been to contextualize, indigenize, and localize what we Anglicans have inherited. The paradox has been to continue to preach, present, and practice a Gospel of Freedom and Human Development, while we still deal with the continuing realities and inclinations of dependence, imitation, and fragmentation still prevalent in our societies.

The diocesan strategy that was adopted for this special celebration was to invite and encourage each island community to celebrate this anniversary in their own way. I hasten to presume that, apart from the feasting, the singing, the praising, and the marching, there must have been some creative ways of not only chronicling the heritage and religious history in each island, but also of collectively assessing what traditions and customs need to be carried forward, as well as those that ought to be left behind. For, it seems to me, we cannot worthily celebrate any social or religious heritage unless we are prepared to repent of those factors and functions that have perpetuated the rigid distinctions to which I have already referred. We would also need to recognize and shore up those strengths and resources, both human and material that have enabled congregations to survive against many odds.

Celebrating our heritage would most certainly involve the acknowledgement of the contributions and sacrifices of innumerable local leaders, both lay and ordained, and missionaries from abroad, over the decades. They have indeed made significant contributions in congregations and communities across the diocese. We should certainly celebrate our heritage, for example, in the field of education, at the primary, secondary and tertiary levels. The Antigua Grammar School and the Antigua Girls High School stand out as prominent examples of Anglican initiatives. We should certainly celebrate the innumerable vocations to the ordained ministry that have been nurtured and sustained over the last century, especially from Anguilla, even though there have been countless episodes of exile, whether voluntary or otherwise. We can certainly celebrate the social, cultural, organizational, and developmental accomplishments among generations of people, even beyond the walls of our churches. Indeed, for most of its existence, the Diocese has struggled to function as an A-B-C Agency – A for Advocacy, B for Beneficence, and C for Compassion. The untiring efforts of Archdeacon Robert Holberton, here in Antigua, and Rev. Daniel Davis in St. Kitts and Nevis around the time of Emancipation, should never be forgotten.

But in celebrating that heritage we should also bear witness to the struggles that local communities have had to engage in, as they have valiantly withstood all the exclusions, indignities, sarcasms, and offenses meted out to them by those who treated us with palpable disrespect and arrogant insensitivity. For example, what is there to celebrate about the fact that a young Anguillan priest was scolded by his English Rector for coming home to the rectory so late that he disturbed the Rector's dog's rest? What is there to celebrate when the wife of that same English priest offered me the rubber bone that the dog would bite on as a suitable toy for my two-month old baby daughter? What is there to celebrate when a Canadian missionary would brazenly exclaim: "That's the trouble with you people; you want Canadian money, but you don't want Canadian ideas!" What is there to celebrate when English missionaries forbade us to call places where our non-Anglican neighbors and friends worshipped "conventicles"; because in their view, they were not "churches"?

Perhaps it all goes back to what was so demographically widespread about the Anglicans in the late 19th century. The laboring classes and the ex-slaves were more readily drawn to the Methodists and the Moravians, rather than the Anglicans. It was generally recognized that the Anglican Church was the religious arm of the local government, as well as the representative body of the 'Mother Country'.

With the obvious social contrast between the Anglican Church on the one hand, and the masses of the people in these parts on the other, what sort of cultural and religious sub-stream could there be to sustain either a legacy of authentic religion, or a noble heritage? "Ecclesiology" is not merely the study of the nature and function of the church as church. It is also the ongoing historical analysis and existential awareness of what the church should really be all about. It is about the continuous assessment of the presumed linkages between what the church preaches and what it practices, together with the conspicuous contradictions and paradoxes between its religious claims and its socio-political proclivities.

At the start of the diocesan structural arrangements in 1842, therefore, the Anglican Church was saddled with several moral, social, political, and cultural contradictions. It was faced with a patent clash of loyalties, whether to God as Creator and Father of everybody, or to the plantocracy, or even to the Gospel of Jesus Christ. How could such competing loyalties co-exist with any degree of progressive outcomes, or ecclesial integrity, or missional authenticity?

Two historical facts must certainly feature into the equation of where the Anglican Church was at the period of the Diocesan inauguration. One had to do with the official end of slavery, and the other with the robust character of the first Diocesan Bishop. As is well known, the British slave trade was abolished some 210 years ago this year, in the year 1807. That is not to say that human trafficking is still not alive and well, and very profitable indeed for any number of persons and groups across the globe. Nevertheless, although the Slave trade was abolished, the system of slavery was not abolished until 1834.

The great debate throughout the West Indies was about the economic, social, and political ramifications involved once the slaves were set free, and they were no longer regarded as the property of the enslavers, or the planters. There was a lively and vicious debate in the Leeward Islands, mainly in Antigua, as to whether the slaves should be set free on August 1ˢᵗ, 1834, or whether they should be placed under a system known as Apprenticeship.

As the debate raged widely and fiercely in Antigua, it was widely reported at the time that the Anglican clergy urged the planters to set the slaves free at once, rather than hold them in a state of semi-slavery for another four years. Most planters were against immediate freedom and were thus bitterly opposed to the Anglican clergy and their stand on the matter. Two planters at the time, Mr. Francis Shand and Mr. Otto Baijer, who owned Ottos Estate, and who were at first in favor of Apprenticeship, changed their minds at the last moment and voted in favor of immediate Freedom. The vote in the Legislative Assembly was tied, and this meant that the Speaker of the Assembly, one Dr. Nicholas Nugent, cast the deciding vote in favor of Freedom. This is perhaps why the name "Nugent" has always been of favorable and noble memory in Antigua.

Apparently, the Anglican clergy convinced those planters that Apprenticeship would be more expensive than Freedom, and that the planters would only be half-owners of the ex-slaves. Mr. Baijer's famous catch phrase was said to have been: "More money, less worry!" In passing, it is well worth noting that Barbados and Jamaica adopted the Apprenticeship system until 1838. It is also worth recalling that the late Dr. Eric Williams had always held to the view, in Caribbean history, that Slavery was abolished not for any humanitarian reasons, but rather for compelling economic reasons on the part of the plantation owners, and the British Government.

The second fact had to do with the embarrassing story surrounding the father of the first bishop of the Diocese. Listen to this excerpt from the book entitled: *Know Your Church*, by Olva Flax: *Certainly the Church of England did not take a positive stand against slavery, in fact some of the clergy were involved in the exploitation of the trade. One notable, if not notorious, example is that of the Revd. William Davis who combined the Rectorship of St. Peter with the attorneyship of the Romney estates in St. Kitts and was arraigned before the Court on a charge of murdering a slave, Eliza. He was acquitted, but it came out in evidence that he was in the habit of disciplining the slaves with his hand or the whip and both. The evidence occasioned great embarrassment to the Governor of St. Kitts and the Secretary of State in England. This incident occurred in the year 1813, and there was a repeat five years later when the Revd. Mr. Rawlins, while acting as Overseer on an Estate killed one of the slaves and on arraignment was found guilty of manslaughter by a lenient jury.* (Olva W. Flax, *Know Your Church,* Antigua Publishing Company, 2000, p.13)

All of this is by way of preface to the character of the first Bishop of the Diocese, Daniel Gateward Davis. He happened to be the son of the same Revd. William Davis who had been acquitted of murder in 1813. Bishop Davis had joined the Movement for the Abolition of Slavery while he was at Oxford and had become a friend of William Wilberforce the great abolitionist. He pioneered the work amongst the slave population especially in Nevis, founding many Sunday schools as Chaplain for the *Incorporated Society for the Conversion and Religious Instruction and Education of the Negro Slaves in the British West Indies.* He pioneered the erection of the famous Cottle Church in Nevis and served as its first Rector. He was also Archdeacon of Antigua from 1835 to 1842.

He had the distinction of winning his legal case for the publishing of banns of marriage for two slaves while he was a Rector in Nevis, and eventually solemnizing their marriage. It was said of him: "As Bishop he is reputed to have proved himself to be a good organizer, diligent in the care of the clergy and people within his jurisdiction and sympathetic with the poorer members of his flock." In 1842, he was consecrated Bishop of Antigua in Westminster Abbey in London on William Wilberforce's birthday, August 24th, St. Bartholomew's Day, which also happens to be the birthday of both my father-in-law and me. (Parenthetically, I made a pilgrimage to Wilberforce's tomb in Westminster Abbey on our joint birthday on the 200th anniversary of the Abolition of the Slave Trade, 2007.) Bishop Davis was enthroned in the ruins of St. John's Cathedral on May 12th, 1843 some 174 years ago this month.

Why was the Cathedral in ruins? Queen Victoria had designated the Parish Church of St. John's as a Cathedral with effect from November 10th, 1842. But there had been a great earthquake on February 8th, 1843 at 10:40 am. It was reported that while the Cathedral bells were ringing in anticipation of the arrival of persons for their wedding ceremony, the whole building was shaken violently, and everyone had to escape for their lives.

Thus, the history of the Diocese of Antigua as a diocese, commenced in a climate of new freedom for ex-slaves, disgruntled and vengeful planters, suppliant priests, self-determined and creative negroes, and harsh economic and geological conditions. During these 175 years therefore, for better or for worse, not only has the climate continued in various forms and systems through patterns of colonialism, post-colonialism, and neo-colonialism, but the Diocesan story itself, as indeed most diocesan stories in the CPWI, has been marked by six main factors. These are continuing factors that link the Heritage of the past, with the challenges involved the seizing the Moment, either through continuities, or discontinuities.

But they also provide a dynamic matrix for either embracing a new Future in this 21st century, or else maintaining and bringing forward the status quo, with all the rites and ceremonies of business as usual. Only time will tell what kind of future this Diocese was ready and willing to embrace at this time, and what steps were put in place to put find new bottles, but not for the old wine. We have already been warned about the dangers of new wine in old bottles, so there is no sense in wasting time, and energy, and money, by trying out that experiment again. It really does not work!

What then are these six factors of which I speak? I choose to list them as follows: *Buildings, Budgets, Benefactors, Bishops, Blessings, and Babies*. These factors not only carry the force of institutional and cultural practices and preferences, they are also endowed with the metaphorical and theological implications that have shaded the ways of collective thinking and individual priorities. It is important to note, however, that any careful review of the various Synod journals and reports, the Charges and Sermons from Bishops, and even some entries from the diaries of Bishop Knowles, which were passed down to me several years ago, would inevitably demonstrate that these six factors were never far from the corridors of diocesan concern. Time does not permit us to expand at length on each of these factors in this presentation but allow me to offer a brief comment on each of them.

First, although it has always been said that the church is not the building, but the people are the church, church people have always placed higher premium and pride on buildings, nevertheless. Churches, rectories, manses, centers, and camping facilities have often consumed and stretched resources of every kind, not least of which have been the pennies of the faithful old ladies. Property issues are always complicated and protracted, but the Church must never find itself putting property above people, for people are heaven-bound, while properties are not. Hurricanes, earthquakes, volcanoes, and other forms of natural disaster have incessantly wreaked havoc on the diocesan story. With the prevailing and constant needs for maintenance and restoration in each territory, the restoration of St. John's Cathedral has obviously suffered from some local anemia and regional malaise. Perhaps it might have been more prudent in the long run to build a new cathedral elsewhere.

Second, Budgets are often constructed as fiscal instruments of operation and obligation, while at the same time they serve to mirror the vision and values of the church, whether at the congregational or diocesan levels. They reflect in very practical tones the priorities of the decision-makers on behalf of the people of God. Because they are mainly comprised of people's extraordinary sacrifices and unimaginable contributive efforts, church budgets need always to be handled as sacred and sacramental trusts, from sources both human and divine. Clumsy hands and careless heads should always be kept far away from scarce church resources, and from areas where people's needs, and human suffering abound. In any event, Diocesan budgets should always be mutually Mission-driven functions of congregational incentivation and empowerment, rather than Maintenance-oriented statutes of central governance and rigid control.

Third, with respect to Benefactors, there is a saying that is not found in the Bible, but which has always enjoyed some quasi-biblical status. It goes like this: "God helps those who help themselves." It has been attributed to Benjamin Franklin. The principle of self-reliance and self-sufficiency is undoubtedly of great value and should always be held in highest esteem. Diocesan dependence on external beneficence and generosity has always been a characteristic in our story, whether it has been for money, manpower, materials, or missionary models. I myself was trained for the ministry at Codrington College with scholarship funds provided by the Anglican Church of Canada. It is my fervent belief, however, that a radical and honest discernment, disclosure, dedication, and deployment of more of our local resources, together with some creative imagination, should go a long way towards eradicating the lingering vestiges of a dependency syndrome among ourselves. It should always be accompanied by a strong and courageous determination to do more with less.

Fourth, I have earlier referred to the various images that Bishops often acquire to themselves. What is not always clear however, is what the faithful people of God require and demand in their bishop as pastoral leader, religious overseer (as in *episcopos*), spiritual mentor, and moral advocate. This diocese has had a variety of episcopal models over these 175 years, ranging from the Majestic and the Militaristic, through the Managerial and the Missional. What is critical for the life of the Church as a whole is to maintain an ongoing sense of nature of the God's Church and its call to Mission, through what is called the *sensus fidelium*, the sense of the faithful people of God, especially through the nurturing and conscientization of those who are called and ordained to lead in our communities of faith. The selection of bishops anywhere should never be a popularity contest. It should rather be a corporate response to a prayerful discernment of a divinely inspired and an authentically assured vocation. We need to remember that there is no known cure for the ecclesiastical disease known as "purple fever".

Fifth, over these 175 years, the Diocese of NECA still has every reason to count its innumerable Blessings. Through all the changing scenes of life, whether in trouble or in joy, God has still been good! Of primary importance among these blessings have been the faith, loyalty, resilience, sustainability, and fortitude of our people. Bishops and priests come and go, but God remains the same. Those who have been rooted and grounded in their faith have never allowed all the infelicities and deficits of treatments and indignities, or the patterns of contempt and arrogance wherever they have occurred, to hold them back from being the church. Hurricanes and earthquakes and other calamites have come and gone, just as much as the surges of crises and conflicts, whether internal or otherwise.

But through it all, the faithful people of this Diocese have held tenaciously to the belief that: "Whom God bless, no man curse". So, they count their blessings, and name them one at a time; for, as they always say, one-by-one will always "full basket". The Diocese must always place the highest possible value on the people in the pews as blessings from God. They are gifts of grace. They are vessels of faith. They are agents of hope. They are icons of love.

Sixth, the Church has had to deal continuously with the challenges and potentials of Babies. The measure of a compassionate society has always been determined by how well it deals with its young and tender ones. Most of the babies born in the Caribbean are born out of wedlock. The Anglican Church has always been challenged in how to minister to unwed mothers and their offspring; and yet, they are all gifts of God, made in God's image. It used to be the practice at St. John's Cathedral to baptize babies born out of wedlock on Fridays, while those born within wedlock were to be baptized on Sundays. Unmarried mothers were not allowed to join the Mother's Union but were accommodated in an organization called the Women's Auxiliary. One may well ask, why are babies a factor in this Diocesan story?

My answer is that it all has to do with the rearing, caring, nurture, and empowerment of those whom God has given to us in procreation. This involves Provision, Protection, Education, Faith and Moral Formation, Civic Investment, Social Upliftment, Family Enrichment, and Career Development, among other things. I hold to the belief that if there are no crying babies, or rumping and stomping infants, or restless youths making their presence felt in the church, then that church is virtually on life-support. Let us never forget that African proverb that says: "Tomorrow belongs for the people who prepare for it today". Another proverb says: "We have not inherited the land from our ancestors, we have only borrowed it from our children." Our babies are us!

So, where do we go from here? What is the "Moment" that we are ready to seize? What shall we bring forward? What shall we abandon as relics, or habits, or patterns of the past? We know where we have come from, and how we have gotten where we are. Do we know where we are heading, and how we plan to get there? I have entitled this presentation: ***NECA AT ONE SEVENTY-FIVE: TO THRIVE, TO THRIVE, OR JUST SURVIVE?*** That is the question. We are thriving along by God's grace and providential protection; but are we thriving just to survive, or are we thriving to move forward and upward as the Church, as the Pilgrim People of God? Are we to be a people on the move, or are we just plain Anglicans saddled with those seven famous Anglican words? Those words go like this: ***We have always done it this way***.

Where will this Diocese be, what will it look like when it celebrates the 200th anniversary, some 25 years from now? What kind of groundwork can we lay now for the next generation of leaders and celebrants, and our offspring yet unborn? This is surely what "Thriving to Thrive" is all about – cultivation, germination, fertilization, nurturing, and pruning – all of those actions spell growth, and change, and creative imagination, and progress, that thrive in bringing forth a vision of the future into our present reality. This is what theologians mean when they call on us to be "proleptic"; we thrive and struggle to create new signs of the Kingdom of God in our midst. Allow me then to offer a few proposals for your further reflection and consideration, in whatever forum or form it might be deemed appropriate so to do. These proposals are being offered within the optic of what I am calling a "Four-D" Analysis. The Four "D's" are: *Discovery, Discernment, Determination, and Deployment.*

Simply put, this Diocese is being called upon to *discover* exactly what it has, in terms of its corporate resources, its practical resolutions, and its potential for congregational growth and institutional refinement. Some would refer to it as "Asset Mapping".

This Diocese is being called upon to *discern* the human talents and social capital that is all around, not only in the pews, but also in the communities of goodwill and patent solidarity, just waiting to be tapped. This would include new modes of discerning those whom God is calling into service, not necessarily for the ordained ministry, but into various forms of witness and fertile fellowship. For let us never forget that those who call themselves into the ordained ministry are not necessarily those whom God has truly called. Divine vocation is a mysterious and complex experience.

This Diocese is being called to *determine* its own theological and moral priorities, for it is only by so doing that its own spiritual, ethical, cultural, and ecclesial polities can be commonly valued and willingly embraced. This would seem to me to be the best way in which the whole family of God might be best encouraged not only to **Know** the Faith, and **Grow** the Faith, but also to **Show** the Faith. After all, therefore we spend millions of minutes and dollars Worshipping, Preaching, and Pastoring.

This Diocese is being called upon to *deploy* its assets, whether spiritual and material, or personal and institutional, in such a way as to reflect its unconditional allegiance to the demands for justice with equality, fairness with diversity, and prudence with efficiency.

Here then, are my suggested proposals.

First, there is an obvious need for a revision of the Diocesan Vision and Mission Statements. These should encapsulate the seriousness of the Diocesan response to the demands of the Gospel of Jesus Christ. They should incorporate the challenges of becoming more and more living signs of the Kingdom of God in these parts. They should also give robust expression to the many tasks of the Church as the Community that is called and convulsed by the power of the Holy Spirit. It is the duty of the Church to turn the world right side up, even if the world would call it upside down.

Second, the Teaching Ministry of the Diocese needs to be taken very seriously as a Vocational Obligation, and not merely as an optional extra. The Gospel speaks of the ministry of Jesus as first, Teaching, then, Preaching, then Healing. A specially trained professional Religious Educator needs to be employed who will coordinate and guide substantive initiatives in Baptismal Covenanting (even for the already baptized), Discipleship Enrichment, Family Life Education, and Transformational Leadership training.

Third, a Digital College for the Laity needs to be established with a great deal of urgency. This College would be commissioned by the Diocese, developed as a Digital Center for training and certification of lay-members young, not so young, and seniors willing to be young again. The training would be in several areas that were deemed essential for the empowerment of the laity and their signal importance in the life of the church. This would go far beyond being adorned in cassocks and cottas and scarfs and reading the lessons in our churches. Catechists could also be trained through this facility.

Fourth, the Church has always been in the vanguard of formal education. Its record of advancing the causes of learning and intellectual development has been unparalleled. But the political directorate has universally assumed that national responsibility. Health Education and Wellness Nurture still beckon the Church into action. Perhaps this is the time for the Diocese to secure and establish partnerships with competent and well-resourced stakeholders in the field of health. Diseases such as Diabetes, Cancer, Dementia, Hypertension, and some other non-communicable diseases, need constant vigilance and education. Each Island Anglican community needs to become prominently involved and committed to this evangelical vocation of "Therapeia", or Healing, as a vital extension of the ministry of Jesus Christ.

Fifth, just as we earlier mentioned Babies as a Diocesan policy factor, so too must our attention to Youth Empowerment and Millennial Engagement become an area of critical importance for the Diocese. This goes way beyond the AYPA (Anglican Young People's Association) Syndrome. It demands a process of listening and learning from the ways of contemporary youths, with all their pain, potential, and prospects for career advancement and responsible citizenship and parenthood. The tyranny of social media, and the captivity of the pervasive drug culture, should drive the Church into an urgent attack on the social enemies of our day, rather than take cover in sanctimonious retreat and sacred obscurity. Our young people are blessed with enormous creativity and artistic imagination; so that time has come for us to release their creativity and dynamism on us. We brought them into the world; we can certainly make room for them to invigorate our lives and stimulate our spirits, before we grow too old to appreciate their invaluable worth and youthful energies.

Sixth, the Diocese must begin to generate a deeper and richer program of Collective Spirituality and Biblical Pastoralia. This would involve the designation of a competently ordained and theologically astute priest to assume this innovative process of enriching the models of Prayer partnerships, Spiritual Enrichment sessions at congregational levels, training programs in Meditative practices and Mindfulness exercises, as well as Biblical reflections on the contextual issues affecting contemporary societies. The Diocese, like the family, that prays together, will certainly grow together.

Finally, the time has come for the formerly known Diocese of Antigua, now known as the Diocese of NECA since 1986, to take some further steps to mark the 175th anniversary It should demonstrate that diocesan culture and institutional life are not geographically stifled. Some new forms of decentralization would give new impetus to the diocesan climate. It is time to designate St. George's Church, Basseterre, and St. Mary's Church, Anguilla as Pro-Cathedrals, with all the rights, rituals and privileges which appertain to such designations. Further, the time has come to locate some diocesan functions in places other than Antigua, perhaps in Nevis or St. Kitts for the time being. In this age of cyber-technology all roads do not have to begin or end in St. John's Antigua.

As the Diocese of NECA draws its celebration of its 175th Anniversary to a close in August, then, there has certainly been much to celebrate, much to repent of, much to restore, and much to renew in our life as the Church of God in this place. As we give thanks for that great cloud of witnesses who have struggled to sustain the face and spirit of Anglicanism, while giving thanks that God is not an Anglican, we can certainly redouble our efforts to bear witness to the unswerving belief that we are not Anglicans who happen to be Christian, but we are Christians who happen to be Anglican. This is the strain in which we bear witness to the faith in that God who has brought us from a mighty long way. God will always be there with us as the Great Emmanuel, to strengthen us for the journey that lies ahead. God still has work for each of us to do in this Great Diocesan Vineyard of Worship, Work, and Witness.

My Dear Sisters and Brothers in the Lord, may we thrive to thrive onwards and upwards, and not settle down with the urges of inertia and mere survival. Allow me then to close with the same words with which I ended an address to the Diocesan Synod some forty-five years ago in 1972: **Let us not think ourselves into a new way of acting; rather, let us act ourselves into a new way of thinking**. May God richly bless us all. THANK YOU.

The Call To Intentional Discipleship

The Diocese of the Bahamas and Turks & Caicos Islands
Nassau, Bahamas, November 2018

I wish to begin by offering you a very famous quotation from the 20th century German martyr Dietrich Bonhoeffer where he is reported to have said that Christianity without discipleship is Christianity without Christ. He bemoaned the fact that while people are ready to claim that they trust in God, they still fail to follow Jesus. Bonhoeffer was also said to have waxed eloquent on the dangers of what he called "cheap grace". He is reported to have said that cheap grace was the mortal enemy of the church.

Let me suggest to you that there is no question in my mind that the primacy of Discipleship in the Christian religion is critical for the unity of the Church, and for the embodiment of the High Priestly prayer of Jesus that we may all be one. The Ecumenism of Discipleship in following Jesus is far more important than the ecumenism of churches and religious groupings. It has been rightly said that while churches are looking for decisions, Jesus is looking for disciples.

Others have said that if a church's strategy is not rooted and grounded in making disciples, the church has abandoned the mission that was given to it by Jesus. We need to respond more fervently to the Invitation of Jesus to follow Him way beyond the regular habit of repeating the Lord's Prayer. Let us explore what this matter of Discipleship is all about.

Generic Discipleship

We need to remember that "discipleship" is not primarily a religious concept even though its usage has been dominated by the religious community, and virtually monopolized by religious discourse. From time immemorial leaders in societies (whether it was in the academy, the public square, business, the professions, religions, or otherwise), always had their followers, their apprentices, their adherents, their learners, their representatives, their vicarious personages, their emulators, their dependents, their pupils. Socrates had his disciples, so too did Aristotle, and Karl Marx, and Joseph Stalin, and Adolf Hitler, and Marcus Garvey, and Bin Laden, and Isis.

So, Discipleship is essentially a way of life, a way of thinking, a way of speaking, a process of personal and personality evolution. It denotes a radical acceptance of the leader's teachings, postures, and example. It generates a deep level of emulation and commitment, and it demands an almost unconditional mode of relationship with the leader or teacher. It calls for a basic prioritization of life principles, personal and social ideals, ideological sensitivities, as well as preferences and choices that seek to advance the causes and vision of a stream of thought and action.

Discipleship is a way of life that spells out one's structure of allegiance, whether it is political, ideological, spiritual, ethical, intellectual, or otherwise. It essentially requires a relentless willingness to learn, to embrace, to follow, and to represent that which is most meaningful in one's life. It generates varying levels of responsiveness both from those within its range as well as those without. Accordingly, it is possible to say that discipleship has the power to ascend to, and assume, the highest levels of human life, and conduct, and dignity, and devotion; while, at the same time, it can plunge into an inexorable descent to the lowest levels of human despair, destruction, and decay. Discipleship can be just as much the engine of terrorism as it can be the energy for spiritual vitality, moral purity, or human ascendancy. A disciple is an avid learner, a radical follower, an embodied symbol, and a committed agent or representative. It all depends on the nature of the leader, and direction of the movement.

It is very important to establish that broad context for our reflections on Discipleship, in general terms, for three very critical and significant reasons. First, human life is about growing, and developing, and changing. Our context, our cultures, our social and material constraints, all combine to delineate what we learn, how we learn what we learn, and what we do with what we learn. In any case, the saying is one hundred percent true: "The more we live, the more we learn!" A disciple is a learner.

Secondly, there are the famous words of St. Paul: *"When I was a child, I spoke like a child, I thought like a child, I reasoned like a child; when I became a man, I gave up childish ways."* (I Corinthians 13: 11 RSV) But do we really put away those things that we call childish, or do we not somehow accommodate our basic personal formation throughout our whole lives, so that we follow instinctively what we have already had ingrained in us? Someone has rightly said that the child is father of the man. We follow our childhood forms. A disciple is a follower.

Thirdly, as we go through life there are innumerable experiences that impact our lives to such an extent that we are sometimes radically converted from one way of life to another, from one mode of behavior to another, or from one type of personality to another. Some may call this revolution; some may call this evolution; some may even call it transformation. Indeed St. Paul calls on his Roman addressees to be transformed by the renewing of their minds; but he does not indicate what might be responsible for triggering such a renewal or transformation. In any evident, change happens; and we are often relocated in places and spaces where we had never been before. We become both changed agents and change agents. A disciple is a changer.

Christian Discipleship

Given these considerations therefore, how do we come to understand and respond to the call for Christian Discipleship in general, and thus for Intentional Discipleship in particular? The Word "Disciple" is mentioned at least 260 times in the New Testament, mainly in the Gospels and the Acts of the Apostles. It comes from the Greek *"mathetes"*, and the Latin *"discipulus"*. They both refer to persons who adhere to, and are committed to, teachings, ethos, doctrines, philosophies of teachers, thinkers, prominent religious figures, either in the past or in the contemporary situations.

The most prominent scenario of Discipleship in the Old Testament is between Elijah and Elisha. Ezra is also named as having disciples. There is a school of thought that the relationship between Moses and Joshua was one of Master-Disciple. There is the mention of the "sons of the prophets" we find in the First Book of Samuel. It is also suggested that the depth and range of the Wisdom literature, particularly in Job, Proverbs, and Ecclesiastes, would not have been sustainable without a group of thinkers and discussants wrestling with some of the deep questions of the day, particularly with respect to moral and ethical issues, and the divine orientation of nature, and the wisdom found in creation.

Outside of the Hebrew Scriptures themselves, there is abundant evidence in Jewish communities that the rabbinical schools had large followings, so that the rabbis themselves were leaders of thought and socio-political activity. This was certainly the context in which Jesus of Nazareth emerged as a prophetic leader and given the title of "Rabboni", by at least two Gospel characters, Bartimaeus in Mark, and Mary Magdalene in John.

Jesus of Nazareth raised the level of discipleship to a very high level. He was obviously very careful in choosing his followers; and this distinguished him from the scenario of John the Baptist and his disciples. The main distinction was that whereas John's disciples chose to follow him of their own volition, Jesus specifically chose his own, and invited them to follow him. What made life even more interesting was that the disciples who first joined the Jesus movement at the invitation of Jesus, then went after other recruits. So, there emerged a dedicated band of followers over time, Matthew, Nathaniel, Phillip, James, John, Martha, Mary, Andrew, and so forth.

In the Acts of the Apostles there is abundant evidence of the diverse range of discipleship in the Apostolic community, and especially with respect to the way in which they were led by the Holy Spirit in bearing witness to the meaning and message of the Jesus Story, particularly after the Pentecost event. There is heightened evidence in the Acts of the Apostles that they understood discipleship to be inextricably linked with the sacred obligation to exercise their missionary zeal. Those who followed Jesus were known to be members of the Way, much more so than members of the Church as such.

Discipleship for them meant a life of movement, and change, and conversion. This gave rise to the fourfold strategy of Evangelism: House groupings, Literature, Missionary activity, and Martyrdom. Discipleship for them involved a life of nurture and compassion, mixed with Christ-centered *kerygma* and God-directed *didache*. It encompassed their dedication of their talents, their gifts, their opportunities, and their special brand of witness with counter-cultural modes of fellowship, and even unjust suffering. The missionary successes of St. Paul would certainly not have been possible without the band of followers and adherents to the Gospel mission who accompanied him and represented him in so many different places.

His farewell address to the church at Ephesus in the Acts of the Apostles has always been one of my favorite passages in the New Testament, spoken by one who was clearly not just a missionary but more importantly a Master Teacher in the tradition of Jesus himself, who remains for all time the Master of the Master-Teachers. At its highest level therefore, Discipleship in the religious key is essentially an inextricable relationship between the Master-Teacher and the Learner. The Learner follows as he/she learns, and bears witness to the transforming changes and growth marks in his/her lifestyle, and in her/his ongoing experiences.

Of course, a critical aspect of the meaning and measures of Discipleship is the obligation to become fully engaged in disciple-making. The classical mandate for this is the so-called Great Commission to go out into all the world and make disciples of all peoples, to and baptize them in the name of the Blessed Trinity. This has always implied that Evangelism, Baptism, and Disciple-making are all integral parts of the same missional and ecclesial mandate. Those who are baptized are expected to live into their commitment to follow Christ, just as much as they undertake to renounce all forms and vestiges of the anti-Christ. This is to be a continuous lifestyle. The Anglican Consultative Council puts it this way: "Being discipled and discipling others is others is a lifelong journey as we follow Jesus Christ, acting on his words, and walking in his ways towards a deeper redeemed relationship with God, being 'changed from one degree of glory to another' as we walk more closely with him and each other." (*Intentional Discipleship*, ACC 2016, p.7)

Varieties of Discipleship

What does it really mean to follow Christ? What does it cost to follow in the apostolic tradition of the Faith once delivered to the Saints? How does the Christian community engage itself in generating new strategies of discipleship-making, as well as discipleship sustaining? Someone once said that it is one thing to go out be fishers of men and women for Christ. But when you catch them you have scale and clean them! If it is true that discipleship is to be about the whole life of the Christian and the Christian community, in the context of our response to the will of God through Christ, what do we do with all of this, and where do we begin to launch out after baptism? The ACC has said that "God's will is that as adults become disciples, so do children, youth, and young adults become disciples of Jesus and disciple-makers, as also those who are differently abled both physically and mentally." (ACC, p.6).

It places demands on family relationships, "the way we handle money, our attitude towards employment and leisure activities, our exploitation of the environment, our political choices, and much more." (ACC, p.6) Issues of culture, sex, power, justice, ecology, friendship, aesthetics, religion, research, and science are all relatable to the basic Christian question of our day; namely, 'Who is Jesus Christ for us today? And what difference does it make?' At the very least, sincere answers to these questions demand a deep measure of spiritual growth, while constantly cultivating such habits of the heart and mind and will that usher into a life of unconditional submission, faithful obedience, and radical dependence on God.

Various religious practitioners have gone to work, and they have come up with an interesting variety of labelling for different approaches to Discipleship. Here are some of them.

Fruitful Discipleship: This is an approach that pays special attention to the fruit of the Spirit as listed in Paul's letter to the Galatians, and it seeks to explicate the meaning and demands of each of these aspects of moral and spiritual growth and development.

Innovative Discipleship: This approach encourages disciples to find new ways of serving Christ beyond the traditional paths of religious forms and formularies. It strives to break new ground in public and social witness, and it emphasizes that there is no place on Earth where Christ cannot be followed, and worshipped, and adored.

Relevant Discipleship: We live in a post-modern world today, and some would even say that it is a post-Christian world. This approach attempts to challenge these labels and assumptions about the times in which we live, and to encourage Christians to take seriously the contemporary contexts in which they find themselves, without seeking to baptize the culture, or to capitulate to its context.

Radical Discipleship: There is always that call to get back to basics and to reclaim that fire of excitement and spiritual commitment that characterized the earliest Christians. This approach will enable Christians to take seriously where and how the Gospel broke into the religious and social sphere. There is always a need to be reminded of what were the original challenges and characteristics involved in following Jesus as the Way, the Truth, and the Life. Taking up the Cross daily and following Jesus is a radical demand for Christian discipleship.

Disruptive Discipleship: I firmly believe that the work of God in the world is always engaged in forms of disruption of human order, and in transforming the patterns and strategies of our human endeavors Disruptive Discipleship involves the radical way of "metanoia", or repentance, a real turning of the world upside down, just as it was described in the Book of The Acts of the Apostles about the witness of the early Christians in Corinth.

<u>Healing Discipleship:</u> The threefold ministry of Jesus is listed in the Gospel as Teaching, Preaching, and Healing. Too often we tend to concentrate on the preaching and the teaching and marginalize the efficacy of the church's healing mission. The therapeutic ministries of the church are often significant for nurture and restoration. Healing Discipleship seeks to emphasize the importance of extending the healing ministry of Jesus.

<u>Narrational Discipleship:</u> This is the direct continuation of the mandate of Jesus to go and tell others what God has done for them. They were to tell their stories to others as a direct form of witness. This form of discipleship is so critical for the spreading of the Word, and for sharing personal and authentic testimonies with one another. Christians must never be reluctant nor ashamed to tell the world what God in Christ continues to do for them, and through them.

<u>Anglican Discipleship:</u> All the varieties that we have just discussed find various expressions in different sectors of our global Anglican family. It is very impressive to observe how Anglicans are free to learn from each other, and to adopt some of the systems and habits of ecclesial culture and religious practices that seem to them be appealing and workable in different settings. This is a clear expression of cross-cultural religious fertilization. For us as Anglicans, Discipleship must be a shared experience and a corporate expression.

The ACC has made certain assertions about Discipleship and Anglicanism. Here they are: 1) Discipleship is the very essence of Anglicanism. 2) Discipleship is the way Anglicans witness to Jesus. 3) Discipleship reflects the Catholic-Protestant nature of the Anglican Communion. 4) Discipleship is the future of the Anglican Communion. 5) Discipleship is the hope of the Anglican Communion. They go on to say that: "It is only through calling all Anglicans, and those who will join as new Christians, to a daily following of Christ that we will avoid error, division, and distraction and know the constant renewal of the Spirit that gives hope for eternity."

Intentional Discipleship

What then is all this talk about Intentional Discipleship after all? What is so special about it? How does this type of Discipleship rise to the level of such prominence? What is it all about, and what does 'Intentionality' entail? The ACC puts it this way: "Intentionality means making a personal relationship with Jesus Christ, who sends us out into the world to be an instrument of God and God's love for and in his world. Life shaped by a personal relationship with Jesus Christ is a life nourished by prayer and study of Scripture, empowered by the Holy Spirit for the life of service (in every sphere of life). One's whole life, with humility, speaks with boldness in witness to one's faith in Christ and his love for the world."

We may well ask: what does Intentionality include? Here are some synonyms for being "intentional": *Being conscious, deliberate, purposeful, willful, knowing, voluntary, set in the way, focused.* Of course, we would do well to remember what some of the opposite attitudes and characteristics are to be intentional. Here is a list of such attitudes: *Being accidental, or haphazard, or hit-or-miss, or random, or aimless, or impetuous, or purposeless, or casual, or "sometime-ish".* All of these are habits and attitudes that militate against Intentional Discipleship.

Intentional Discipleship demands of us those strong spiritual and moral tests that I mentioned in this church last Sunday morning. Intentional Discipleship demands real gravitas, real substance, real depth of personhood. This involves a constant surge of intelligent faith, and study, and search, not only in the Scriptures, which is non-negotiable, but also in the ways of God's world into which we are sent to bear witness and to redeem.

Intentional Discipleship demands real Sacrifice of ourselves, offering up to God that which is most precious and valuable, whether in our own eyes or in the eyes of the world. What we attempt to do for God's sake is invariably blessed by the providential grace of God to reap benefits and opportunities, far beyond our wildest imagination or expectations. I believe that genuine sacrifice always leads to divine success; if we allow God to measure that success in God's terms and not ours. Remember that God does not call us to be successful, God simply calls us to be faithful; and in doing so, we can always trust in the trustworthiness of God. So, the miracle of feeding in all the four Gospels is central and pivotal to the Jesus Story, as well as in our own. God always has the means of making our little genuine sacrifices to go a very long, long way.

Intentional Discipleship demands the highest level of personal authenticity and the deepest level of genuine Sincerity. Such a demand requires of us that level of trust in God, where we are always seeking to be converting to Christ, over, and over again. It is the constant replay of our baptismal promise: Do you turn to Christ? The answer is: I turn to Christ every day. Sincerity demands a spiritual curiosity, a spiritual openness to God's Spirit, and the convulsive effects that will take hold of us, in season and out of season. It demands a spiritual quest to seek for Christ not only in our own encounters with each other, but also in the deep searchings and longings of our own hearts, and minds, and wills.

The path of Intentional Discipleship leads us inexorably from the point of Need through the point of seeking through a fervent and regular prayer-filled lifestyle. We can reach the point of finding God afresh day after day, and through our resolute determination to follow Christ, even in moments, and places, and spaces where we would rather not go. So, it demands of us that constant obedience to the will and ways of Christ, that radical sense of kenosis and self-denial for the sake of Christ, and that utter, complete, and unconditional dependence on God's unmerited grace. What more do we want?

Finally, Intentional Discipleship is a shared experience. We journey on this pilgrimage of faith together, always reminding ourselves to get rid of all excess baggage. We believe together. We are called up together both individually and collectively. We bear each other's burdens. We uphold each other in divine love, in prayer, with compassion, with generosity, in the clinics of mercy and justice, and with the joy of mutual support and inexhaustive forgiveness. Someone has rightly said that "Discipleship is a call to 'me' but is a journey of 'we'".

Here then are Fifteen flashpoints to ponder and treasure: Five from the New Testament; Five Marks of Intentional Discipleship in addition to all that we have shared in this presentation; and Five Divinely Blessed Rings for your holy fingers.

Five NT Passages: (Revised Standard Version)
1) **Philippians 2: 5-11**
2) **Mark 1: 14-20**
3) **John 1: 43-51**
4) **Romans 12: 1-5**
5) **Galatians 6: 14-18**

Five Marks of Intentional Discipleship
1. **The Call**
2. **The Cost**
3. **The Courage**
4. **The Charism**
5. **The Contagion.**

Five Divinely Blessed Rings for Holy Fingers
FAITH, FREEDOM, FORGIVENESS, FELLOWSHIP, FUTURE.

Let me close then with words of invitation, assurance, and encouragement from St. Paul: He begins Chapter 8 of Romans with these words: *"There is therefore now no condemnation for those who are in Christ Jesus."* (Romans 8:1 RSV) In other words, you have nothing to be afraid of, and nothing to be ashamed of, in being Intentional Disciples. But listen to how he ends that same Chapter: *"For I am sure that neither death, nor life, nor angels, nor principalities, nor things present, nor things to come, nor powers, nor height, nor depth, nor anything else in all creation, will be able to separate us from the love of God in Christ Jesus our Lord."* (Romans 8:38,39 RSV).

My Dear Sisters and Brothers, that is good enough for me, and I trust that it is good enough for you as well. AMEN.

The Anglican Mission Of Christ –
Marks, Mandate, and Movement

A Paper delivered to the Synod of the Diocese of The Winward Islands, in St. George's, Grenada October 16ᵗʰ – 21ˢᵗ, 2016

T hose who profess to be followers of Jesus Christ are at one and the same time members of the Body of Christ, missionaries of the Gospel of Christ, and witnesses to the faith and hope of the Risen Christ. Because the Church is essentially the Community of the Risen Christ, it is also the Community of the Spirit of the Risen Christ, and the Community with the Mandate from the Risen Christ. Why is this emphasis on the Risen Christ so critical for our understanding of the Mission of Christ – the *Missio Christi*? The answer is threefold.

First, the Resurrection faith stands at the very center of the Christian's understanding of God, and the affirmation of the Jesus Story. The God who is, is the God who became incarnate in Jesus Christ. This is a unique and distinguishing claim for us as Christians; especially as the very notion of the Divine (God's) existence has taken on a fleshly and historical form, with all the inherent characteristics of human life and historical reality. Human life emerges, it expands, and it expires. The Christian Creed confesses that the historical Jesus emerged (born), expanded (grew), and expired (died); but Death was not the end. God raised Him up, we profess. That is why in the very heart of our Eucharistic moment we re-affirm our faith with the words: *Christ has died, Christ is Risen, Christ will come again.* In that uniquely Christian acclamation, our faith enables us to link the past, with the present, and the future. We should never take those words lightly in our common and regular worship.

Second, the Resurrection faith assures us of that critically significant meaning of the Real Presence of Christ in our midst. Every Christian is to be engaged in practicing the art of the Presence of Christ. We are to live out the meaning of our Baptism. We are to fully activate the power and purpose of our prayers. We are to respond to the urgings of the Spirit of Christ, even sometimes in ways of which we are not fully aware. We are to gather to worship, fellowship, and reason collectively in the Name of Christ. We are to acknowledge with humility that it is only by the grace of God in Christ that we are who we are, and we do what we do in Christ's Name. In these and in so many other ways, the mystical presence of the Risen Christ is what empowers, enlivens, and engages the Christian community in what it seeks to do, to transform, and to become, in the face of a world that would rather that the Church just faded out of existence.

To fight against this worldly desire (that the Church should just get out of the way), is what has sustained the Church for nearly 2000 years. Martyrdom and Mission have always gone hand in hand to ensure that the Resurrection Faith was not merely preached and praised, but also practiced and prolonged. So, if the saying is true that the "blood of the martyrs is the seed of the Church", the question is: where is that blood today, and in whose veins does it flow? Martyrdom is not necessarily about dying; it is essentially about living out what we fervently believe, without any fear of dying for that Faith.

Third, the Resurrection faith not only inspires and reinforces the sacrificial solidarity of Martyrdom – whether ancient or modern, whether historical or existential – it also gives life and meaning to the cruciality of Mission. It is rooted and grounded in our basic understanding of the nature of God. The God who is, is the God who comes. The God who comes, is the God who calls. The God who calls, is the God who empowers. The God who empowers, is the God who sends. The God who sends, is the God who sustains and supports. The God who sustains, is the God who receives. The God who receives, is the God who sends again, and again, and again. Mission is not simply a divine agenda – it is more distinctly a Divine Function. Nowhere is this made clearer than in the roots of our Trinitarian affirmation. God sends forth God's Spirit, not only to bring Creation into being, but also to renew the face of Creation. In the fullness of time, says the writer of the Letter to the Hebrews, God sends His Son.

This is the crux of the Resurrection Faith; for in the story of the Upper Room experience, the Risen Christ exercises his Trinitarian mission. He breathes on his timid and bewildered friends and empowers them with the Holy Spirit. The Mission of God is the Mission of Christ. The Mission of Christ is the Mission of the Spirit. The Mission of the Spirit is the Mission of the Church. The Mission of the Church is its Mark, its Mandate, and its Movement.

The centrality of the Easter Message cannot be overstated either in our Christian discourse, or our Christian decision-making, or more particularly in our Christian witness. It is that alone that makes us unique in our understanding of who God is, what God does, and what God expects of us. It is that alone that empowers us to withstand all the surges of nothingness that confront us in our daily existence. It is that alone that undergirds our reason to hope in the face of increasing hopelessness. It is that alone that strengthens our resolve to keep on keeping on, even when the justification for doing so might appear weak and unreasonable. It is that alone that can enlist our full and unconditional engagement in God's work of bringing chaos out of human order.

Easter Faith is about transformation and Renewal. Easter Faith is about Redemption and Liberation. Easter Faith is about Re-imagining and Re-branding. Easter Faith is about new Meaning for life, and new Movement for Mission. So, the disciples run with the Message of Easter even if they have not been witnesses of Easter. The Message is powerful enough for them to spread the Word that they had seen The Risen Lord. They spread it with their faith. They spread it with their experiences. They spread it with their skills. They spread it with their blood. It has been that relentless spreading of the Easter Message that has brought us to this point of our human existence, our human experiences, our human expressions, and our human expectations.

As people of Easter Faith two pivotal questions persist: What does God expect from us? What do we expect from God? Just as God continues to snatch Life out of the jaws of our death-making cultures and conditions, so too does God continue to demand of us that unconditional response and resolve to embrace God's Mission, Christ's

Message, and the Spirit's Movement. For as many as are led forth by the Spirit of God, they indeed are the children and missionaries of God. Accordingly, the children of God are called "Disciples". Discipleship demands intentional loyalty and radical obedience, just as much as it demands total commitment and unwavering consistency.

This is particularly true for us Anglicans as Christians. May we never forget what our identifying mark is as Anglicans. We are not Anglicans who happen to be Christians. Rather, we are Christians who happen to be Anglican. As quiet as it is sometimes kept, let us never forget that the God of the Anglicans is not an Anglican! Nevertheless, as Anglicans, we are committed by our Baptism to live out the marks of our incorporation into Christ and His Church. We are sustained by the Mission of Christ, and the Mission of Christ provides for us our Mandate. There are some Marks of Mission that should activate our imagination.

Marks of Mission

We Anglicans are famous throughout the global religious community for our plethora of consultations, conferences, synods, commissions, and festivals and processions, and luncheons. They signify the importance that we attach to getting together, talking together, planning together, and pronouncing together. Although the Anglican Communion is only the third largest grouping of Christians in the world (Roman Catholics first, and Orthodox second), it is more than likely that we produce more documents and pronouncements per capita than any other religious body in the world. The Anglican challenge has always been to follow through on the resolutions, agreements, canons, and other conventions that we promulgate. This is not to urge us to descend into sacred cynicism; it is rather to urge us on to become who we claim to be, to do what we agree to do, and to go where God has called us to go.

This consideration is particularly relevant to documents and pastoral letters that emerge from CPWI synods, and conventions, and "House" meetings, just as much as it does to global documents and pronouncements from the Anglican Communion as a whole. As early as 1984, the Anglican Consultative Council agreed on what it called the "Five Marks of Mission", and these marks have been re-affirmed at various meetings and conventions ever since then.

The question has always been, are these marks points of departure, or are they processes of a movement, or are they in fact points of arrival? Do they shape a vision of what it means to be Anglican, or do they set the agenda for what Anglicans are likely to use to assess their role and place in God's Vineyard? Whatever the answers might be, they can, at the very least, provide us with a paradigm for corporate witness and personal mission. The five "Marks" are as follows: (1) To proclaim the Good News of the Kingdom. (2) To teach, baptize and nurture new believers. (3) To respond to human need by loving service. (4) To transform unjust structures of society, to challenge violence of every kind and pursue peace and reconciliation. (5) To strive to safeguard the integrity of creation and sustain and renew the life of the earth.

While it is true that these five marks contain all the noble ideals of building civil society, and all the ingredients that can spur the pursuit of the Common Good, and all the central values of Christian witness and service, they merely provide us with empty shells that still need to be filled with meaning and movement. Twentieth century Anglican history was replete with a surge of elegant catch phrases. Some of these included the following: "Mutual Responsibility and Interdependence", "Partners in Mission", "Bonds Of Affection", "Decade of Evangelism". The contemporary challenge is for Anglicans to ensure that in the present century, "Marks of Mission" does not earn its place on the shelves of Anglican archival impotence. The challenge is for each sector of the global Anglican family to comprehend, to contextualize, and to communicate the essential Mandate to which these Marks seek to give full, faithful, and fervent concrete expression in both corporate and personal witness. What then is the Mandate that can give life and full meaning to these Marks?

The Mandate of the Gospel

As we return to the Easter Drama in that Upper Room, we recall the greeting of "Peace" (Shalom) which the Risen Christ proffered to the assembled disciples. Not only did he breathe on them the outpouring of the Spirit of God, he also commissioned them to become Apostles. Having done that, he further charged them to take up where his own ministry had left off, namely, that they were to forgive the sins of all who were penitent. The very first Mandate that the Risen Christ gave to his Church, the Apostolic Community, was the responsibility to proclaim and practice the mystery, message, and meaning of God's forgiveness.

Accordingly, the Church of Christ, Anglicans included, is committed to the mission, ministry, and movement of God's forgiveness. It is mainly in that mode of its existence and witness that the Church must always understand its very reason to be, and its mandate to become what it was called to be. It also struggles in multiple ways to mediate the meaning of the Kingdom of God, and also to market the efficacies of its mandate. Here then are the central characteristics of the Mandate of Christ's Gospel:

1. *To be reconciling Agents of salvation through the proclamation and practice of God's Forgiveness*

2. *To nurture God's people by feeding them with the Word of Life and the Bread of Life*

3. *To promote the Common Good so that all may come to a clearer knowledge of the creative love of God*

4. *To strengthen the faithful in their pilgrimage, and to remove all hindrances which might cause them to stumble*

5. *To bear constant witness to the Good News of Christ through worship, preaching, teaching, healing, and service*

6. *To fight against the forces of Evil, in any and every form, seeking always to overcome Evil with Good*

7. *To become agents of healing and instruments for the reversal of human brokenness*

8. *To promote, provide, and proclaim fresh grounds of hope in the face of constant despair*

9. *To explore, experiment, express, and experience wholesome community as a shared reality of faith in the Risen Christ*

10. *To join with all who confess the Name of Christ in the celebration of life's journey towards God, with Christ, through the Spirit.*

Caribbean Anglican Movements for the Mission of Christ

What then are the Caribbean Marks of Mission that will enable Caribbean Anglicans to live out the Mandate of the Gospel, implement the Global Marks of Mission, and bear fervent witness to the Easter Faith that binds all Christians in common cause? Above all, what are some of the compelling challenges of our times that would transform us and our fellow pilgrims from being "Easter pieces" into becoming genuine "Easter agents"?

Allow me to offer some special Anglican themes and thoughts which might hopefully stimulate some further dialogue and reflection beyond the time constraints of this session. Here they are:

1. Anglicans are the nurture and be nurtured by Word and Sacrament, empower and empowered by God's Spirit, and enliven and enlivened by the Love of God.

2. While Anglicans maintain their traditional Quadrilateral of Scripture, Sacraments, Creed, and Apostolic Ministry, they are responsible for creating and promoting their Contextual Trilateral of Worship, Work, and Witness. The Four and the Three must travel together with fervent vitality.

3. Anglicanism must be driven and sustained as a Movement of the Future and not a Monument of the Past.

4. The Anglican Tradition is rightly characterized as being Catholic, Evangelical, and Reformed. We need to build on that third characteristic to make its Reform as a principle and praxis of growth and change in response to the Kairos in the Mission of Christ.

5. Listen to the late Archbishop Michael Ramsey: *For while the Anglican church is vindicated by its place in history, with a strikingly balanced witness to Gospel and Church and sound learning, its greater vindication lies in its pointing through its own history to something of which it is a fragment. Its credentials are its incompleteness, with the tension and travail of its soul. It is clumsy and untidy, it baffles neatness and logic. For it is not sent*

to commend itself as the 'best type of Christianity', but by its very
brokenness to point to the universal Church wherein all have died."
(Gospel & Catholic Church, 1936, p.220)

Anglicanism should be treated as a branch of Christianity and not just a denomination. It must continue to develop and sustain its own Culture, its own range of Concourse and Communion, as it manages itself as a Global Corporate Reality. While the Liturgy must remain central to its corporate life and conduct, Anglicanism must become a stronger leader in the broader spheres of Ministry – namely, the Pastoral, the Prophetic, and the Practical. Anglicanism must continue to actively pursue the fuller meaning of its famous phrase, "Via Media". It is no longer valid to maintain that principle as an internal mode of discipline and order. "Via Media" must be activated beyond the realm of Theology, and focus more intentionally on Sociology, Anthropology, Ecology, Economics, and Human Technology. The more we know about ourselves and our world is the more we ought to know what to do and how to do it. Anglicanism has a critical role to play in this era diversity, uncertainty, and ethical calamity.

It is to be hoped that Caribbean Anglicans will make haste to engage in the Movement of Missional Implementation. The times are urgent; the days are evil; and the darkness is upon us. The extension of the Incarnation of Christ is a badge of the Christian Church. This extension involves the Message of Christ, the Mission of Christ, and the Movement of Christ as well. The sense of urgency is reminiscent of the Easter Drama that is symbolized by the image of the Empty Tomb. For, while we live in a world that desperately tries to refill its empty tombs and therefore pushes our lives, our values, and our divine rights to be fully human, towards the tombs of death and decay, the movement of our Easter Faith is for us, as Anglicans, to run away from the Empty Tomb, and to confront the death-making challenges of our culture, our contexts, and our countries. As Easter people we know that the Stone has been rolled away.

The Caribbean continues to be saddled with moral, spiritual, social, political, economic, and environmental challenges, just as much as any other region in the world. It is cold comfort to claim affiliation with other regions of the world that are experiencing similar challenges. It is for us to examine very carefully and prayerfully the root causes, the attendant ripple effects, as well as the modes of confrontation that can be engaged locally, nationally, and regionally. Challenges of Poverty, Cultural alienation and imitation, External Influences, Dependence, and Fragmentation persist in the region. Human trafficking, Drug trafficking and consumption, Domestic violence and abuse, Family reconfigurations, and Institutional Injustices all assault the human condition in the region. Cries for Justice – whether Reparatory, Economic, Restorative, or Distributive – are rising more eloquently, coupled with the rising expectations of our youth to whom we have given life; but we have not found for them enough bread.

Let the Anglican Movement of the Easter Faith as the Mission of Jesus Christ continue! For if God be for us, who can be against us????

Section Four

The Romney Moseley
Inaugural Lectures

Trinity College, Toronto, Canada

A THEOLOGICAL RECONSTRUCTION OF THE MYTH OF MULTICULTURALISM

As this millennium draws to its close, this twentieth century leaves behind an unwholesome list of human anathemas in the context of an impressive list of human accomplishments. Never in the history of humankind have so many awesome wins been overcome by so many awful losses. As we have scaled the commanding heights of our human endeavors, we have also plumbed the depths of inhumanity and shame. Nowhere has this historical contradiction been in greater evidence than in the field of cultural encounters and human difference.

This has been the century of two world wars, in which human blood was spilt in unprecedented torrents for the feeble gains of a few, and that by people who were the great inheritors of the Age of Enlightenment. The great surges of the human mind did not in any way deter the rushing onslaught of the brutal spirit. War became a badge of honor in a way that human history had never heralded it before, and with that badge, there hung the unseemly pride of one group's dominance over another. It was not the greatness of the human race that counted. It was rather the presumed greatness of one ethnic or ideological clan over others.

Culture, that sum total of the creative human spirit, (to use Paul Tillich's definitional approach) was overtaken by the sum total of the insatiable human appetite for dominance and control. So the rise of the Iron Curtain, the designation of global partitions – First World, Second World, Third World – the emergence of a new vocabulary for the global family to be deployed along lines of development or underdevelopment, all placed the picture of a mosaic of human cultures under the inglorious shadow of brutal evil and social injustice.

The global conflagration of human contempt made way for the tragic holocaust of the modern sons and daughters of Zion. The Aryan race was to reign supreme; and the rest of the world almost found itself unable to abort such a design. The sons and daughters of Africa, having been driven from the places of their umbilical rootage, were subjected to apartheid and imperialism in the name of God, to decimation and deceit in the name of freedom, and to further balkanization and brutality in the lust for power. All of this was mainly because of their proximity to the beasts of the field and the fowls of the air, and the fruit and color of the land. It was mistaken for poverty, and not for power, for backwardness and not for beauty. Most recently, the term "ethnic cleansing" has emerged with brutal force and evil vigor, as the European infamous brand of fear and hatred, so widely felt throughout the globe, has now turned inwards on itself.

Throughout this twentieth century, a period that has already been claimed by *Time* magazine as the American century, the United States of America has emerged as the richest, the strongest, the brightest, and the only super-power left in the world. And yet, it has been unable to make full use of its wonderful opportunities of developing the incredibly rich human potential of all its citizens. While it has maintained its national allegiance to the idea of constitutional democracy, it has also found itself unable to live into the spirit of its founding documents and declarations about all humans being created equal, about the pursuit of liberty and happiness for all, or the full enjoyment of equality before the law.

More than a century-and-a-quarter after the official abolition of slavery, people of African descent are still waiting to exhale. They wait in hope. But some wait with fear. They are not overcome by the fear of being black. They are confronted with the fear of being "un-White", for that condition still seems to justify "hi-tech lynching", racial profiling, social exclusion and territorial red-lining, biased medical attention, violent hate crimes, church-burnings, industrial exploitation, and judicial contempt. Whether it is in the United States, Brazil, or elsewhere, black people remain the only race of humans in world history whose claim to being fully human has still not been consistently, fully, or universally acknowledged.

At the end of this millennium therefore, the New World, which was so imaginatively inaugurated in the middle of the fifteenth century, has still not established a new-world-order of freedom and justice for all. Furthermore, the vestiges of human enslavement, systemic holocaust, ethnic cleansing, and racial apartheid have yet converged, and they are still embodied somewhere in the lives of our people of color. Racism is still very much alive and well. People of color are still struggling to refute lingering notions that they are the "wretched of the Earth" (Fanon). Multiculturalism has appeared as the myth of all myths, with its promise of human virtue and social equality. But racism does not languish. It runs and is not weary. It walks and is not faint.

There are voices in the other so-called minority communities who express grave doubts about the meaning and motives behind official multiculturalism. Some see it as an attempt of the dominant culture to co-opt the dominated among them into accepting their ideas and ways as normative. There are those who see it as a colossal attempt to cover over the inequities of the society, and a not-so-subtle effort to postpone the inevitable task of reconstructing a more just and human society. Nevertheless, it must also be borne in mind that it is not only people who are blessed with ebony grace (people of color, black people) who express grave reservations and cynical resistance to the meaning and effects of multiculturalism.

A very useful discussion on this distinction has been provided for us by Professor Charles Taylor of McGill University in his essay: "The Politics of Recognition", published in a book entitled *Multiculturalism* (Amy Gutmann ed., *Multiculturalism*, Princeton University Press, New Jersey 1994). Taylor's essay provides the basis for a wide-ranging discussion by several scholars in that book. His main thesis is that *"our identity is partly shaped by recognition or its absence, often by the misrecognition of others, and so a person or group of people can suffer real damage, real distortion, if the people or society around them mirror back to them a confining or demeaning or contemptible picture of themselves. Nonrecognition or misrecognition can inflict harm, can be a form of oppression, imprisoning someone in a false, distorted, and reduced mode of being." (p.25)* He offers the distinction between the politics of equal dignity in which "what is established is meant to be universally the same, an identical basket of rights and immunities"; and the politics of difference in which the unique identity of each individual or group is recognized, as well as their distinctness from everyone else.

In calling for a politics of equal respect, Taylor suggests that there must be something "midway between the inauthentic and homogenizing demand for recognition of equal worth, on the one hand, and the self-immurement within ethnocentric standards, on the other. There are other cultures, and we have to live together more and more, both on a world scale and commingled in each individual society."(p.72) Towards the conclusion of his essay, Taylor suggests that the presumption of equal worth is the way in which we ought to approach others. He ends with these very powerful words: *There is perhaps after all a moral issue here. We only need a sense of our own limited part in the whole human story to accept the presumption. It is only arrogance, or some analogous moral failing, that can deprive us of this. But what the presumption requires of us is not peremptory and inauthentic judgments of equal value, but a willingness to be open to comparative study of the kind that must displace our horizons in the resulting fusions. What it requires above all is an admission that we are very far away from that ultimate horizon from which the relative worth of different cultures might be evident. This would mean breaking with an illusion that still holds many 'multiculturalists' – as well as their most bitter opponents – in its grip."* (p.73)

Throughout the discussion in this book, there is a constant concern for the meaning of freedom in the face of difference, and the primacy of equal rights and human dignity. Multiculturalism must deal with the tensions between personal and collective identities, between the rights of the individual, the obligations of the state, and the mutual affirmation of each other's claims to full development and social support. Gutmann reminds us that a multicultural society *is bound to include a wide range of respectable moral disagreements, which offers us the opportunity to defend our views before morally serious people with whom we disagree and thereby learn from our differences. In this way, we can make a virtue out of the necessity of our moral disagreements.* (p.22) In other words, all horses cannot, and do not have to run alike; and that's all right. Gutmann suggests that the "moral promise of multiculturalism depends on the exercise of" mutual respect for reasonable intellectual, political, and cultural differences. These are the deliberative virtues on which the freedom and equality of all people must rest.

The search for the common good is always pursued beyond the realm of cultural accidents or ethnic heritage. So that even multiculturalism, when it is pursued as an end in itself – its many glittering promises notwithstanding – is always more than likely to be found wanting in the courts of freedom, truth, love, and justice. These are eternal verities that incessantly transcend the limits of any culture and carry their power beyond the reach of any political or strategic manipulations. So, there is multiculturalism by *decree*. There is multiculturalism by *design*. There is multiculturalism by *default*. Some say that there is also multiculturalism by *decay*. But there is also multiculturalism by *"Dee Lord"*. It is to that approach to the myth of multiculturalism that I now invite you to turn our attention.

Towards A Theological Reconstruction

To say that people are more than their cultures is perhaps too simplistic an assertion; but I think that it is nevertheless true. Although our cultures pre-date us and post-date us, there is something more to being human that culture itself does not and cannot define. As human beings we have the capacity to create and pro-create, to adjust and to discern adjustments, to communicate and to respond to others. For each one of us, we are always conscious of the fact that there is much more to us than meets the eye. Our cultures are aggregates of our values and meaning, and these are often embodied in material objects, or social mechanisms such as ritual, ceremonies, and customs.

Cultures then are descriptions of people, and groups of people, but they have no independent existence, even if you might smell my curry from afar, or hear my reggae music in the neighborhood. By their very nature, cultures spell diversity. Cultural diversity is itself not merely an inescapable fact, it is more particularly an authentic sign of God's creative design. For the Christian, there is no human being that represents the possibility of a divine creative mistake. The life-giving

God who chooses to create in the divine image, is also the life-saving God who chooses to re-create with divine freedom. Cultural diversity then, is a living symbol of God's sovereignty and God's love.

It is this basic reaffirmation of the nature of God, this constant acknowledgment that God is known by what God does, which should form the basis of any theological reconstruction of the myth of multiculturalism for the Christian community. The critical challenge for the Christian is to resist the temptation of holding God under the siege of any culture, or of refusing God a work permit in sectors of humanity beyond our control, or even of excommunicating from God's love and compassion those who are different from us. As long as we are prepared to allow God to remain unconditionally free, and to become engaged in a relationality from which no one is excluded, then our understanding of God's trinitarian love will be enriched, and our faithful response to that love will embrace cultural diversity as a blessing and not as a personal threat, nor a social curse.

For to speak of God as Trinity, Father, Son, and Spirit, or Creator, Liberator, and Sustainer, is not merely to affirm that there is plurality in the Godhead, or that God is made known in creation through diversity, but also to acknowledge that we are who we are because God is God to us, at least three times, but in a different way. The God who is making us, is also the God who is saving us, and still the God who is trying hard to sanctify us or keep us holy. But that is a hard job, chiefly because of our relentless abuse of our freedom, and our insatiable thirst for power over others. Multiculturalism as a human myth then, is not antithetical to the human lust for power, and may even be pursued as a collective determination to define and control others, unless it is answerable to a higher order of moral and spiritual imperative. I choose to call that imperative "**Transculturalism**".

Based on our trinitarian understanding of God and God's love, then, Transculturalism emphasizes not a diversity-in-unity motif, but a unity-in-diversity. It calls us to a fresh understanding of what is meant by the Gospel proclamation of the Kingdom of God, or the Realm of God. For that Realm of God is that which cuts aslant across everything by which we seek to define and be defined and calls us out of our self-centeredness into a radical fellowship and solidarity with the others. It worships at no one's altar, neither does it exalt any national or ethnic heritage. Transculturalism offers us a fresh understanding of the world in which God has placed us at such a time as this, and invites us to construct a new cosmology in which, far from seeking to dominate or destroy our world, God's holy and created order, we seek to embrace the richness of its variety and opportunity for making humanity fully human.

Transculturalism takes very seriously the manifesto of Jesus that he had come that all might have life and have it in all its fullness. He did not come that some might have more life than others. The truly Christian anthropology will always insist that the human agenda is infinitely more important than the cultural agenda. Professor Steven Rockefeller put it this way: "Our universal identity as human beings is our primary identity and is more fundamental than any particular identity, whether it be a matter of citizenship, gender, race, or ethnic origin."(*Multiculturalism*, p.88)

Transculturalism is the means by which the church is called to be the church. That is to say, if it is truly to be that community of faithful response to the call of God in Jesus Christ, a community of reconciliation and forgiveness, a community of diverse gifts and graces, a community of gracious and courageous hospitality, a community of resurrection from the death of evil and alienating sin, a community of hope and salvation in our history, then let the church be the church. This is the community in which everything is to be turned upside down.

The meek are to inherit the earth. The poor are to fill the Kingdom of Heaven. Those who hunger and thirst for justice are to be satisfied. The mourners are to be comforted. It is to be the one, holy, apostolic, and catholic community, in which its members are led by the Pentecostal Spirit that speaks one language in many accents. And that language is not English. It is the language of love; not the love of power, but the power of love, which can set all of us free from the slavery of our difference. *"For freedom, Christ has set us free, stand fast therefore, and do not submit again to a yoke of slavery."* (Galatians 5:1 RSV). These are the words of St. Paul the great transculturalist of our Christian tradition. The catholicity of the church is not merely to be interpreted as a multicultural mark, but rather as a dynamic divine vocation to be a universal and faithful witness to God's saving love and uncompromising justice.

What then are some of the moral, theological, and practical implications for a personal and corporate life of Christian Transculturalism? How can it reconstruct that contemporary myth of multiculturalism, and perhaps rescue it from some of the shadowy spheres of human self-interest? How can we help to further ensure that social policies, however well-intentioned, do not treat human beings as means to other ends, but respect the freedom, worth, and dignity of every human being? Allow me to suggest a few theological proposals as theses, perhaps, for further reflection and debate.

One. The sustained development of an inter-cultural theological curriculum is central to the process of theological formation, liturgical renewal, and Christian social engagement. Emphasis only on traditional Western modes of theological reflection and exposition is both intellectually monological and theologically malnourishing.

Two. The promotion of an *ethic of the person* is essential to counter-act the *ethos of the personality*. Personhood is concerned with **who I am**, but personality is only concerned with **what I am and what I do**. Transculturalism focuses on the meaning of persons, while multiculturalism focuses on the social and market value of personalities. Persons have character, but personalities have only characteristics.

Three. The Church is not merely a community of communities, it is also a community, a *koinonia* of gifts, or *charisms* (charismata). These gifts are known to us as "spiritual gifts", or gifts of the Spirit. We need to develop in our churches practical ways of discerning each other's gifts, and the ways in each they can be acknowledged, encouraged, and made available to the whole body of Christ. Transculturalism empowers us to accept cultural gifts as spiritual gifts.

Four. The proclamation of the Gospel is incomplete without the Gospel *praxis*. There are some Gospel imperatives which are crucial for the Church's life and witness in the society. These insist that the Gospel must be a concrete social instrument of the six 'E's: *Equality, Excellence, Efficiency, Enlightenment, Enjoyment, Exchange.* Transculturalism urges us to take these movements of the human heart seriously, and to lift every soul to the highest level of their divine potential.

Five. In the context of an aggressive multicultural thrust in any society, there is inevitably an unwholesome encounter between the weak and the strong, the rich and the poor, the powerful and the powerless, the nationals and the foreigners, the late-comers and the long-timers, the insiders and the outsiders. The church is called to be the prophetic community that is seized by a divine call in the crisis of the historical moment. It must leave no stone unturned in protecting the unprotected, in proclaiming truth to power. It must make no overtures to become a suppliant guest in Pharaoh's court. For Jesus is not only the Christ of God, he is also the New Moses, the Liberator.

Six. The church is not merely the promoter of sacred speech, whether in prayer, or praise, or proclamation, it is also to be the generator of a distinctly moral vocabulary for the whole society. Transculturalism does not thrive merely on multilingualism, it also offers to the society a new grammar, a new level of discourse that is driven by the moral virtues of justice, freedom, truth, equal rights, human dignity, and inexhaustible compassion. We must fight valiantly against negative stereotypes of any culture and affirm the full beauty of what it really means to be human, even among those who might yet be termed "the least of these".

The language of heaven must become the language of the church, and there are no outcasts in heaven. For God is the Supreme Transculturalist. Paul put it this way in Acts 17:26-28 (RSV) *"And he made from one every nation of men to live on all the face of the earth, having determined allotted periods and the boundaries of their habitation, that they should seek God, in the hope that they might feel after him and find him. Yet he is not far from each one of us, for 'In him we live and move and have our being'.*

In spite of its historical revolution against the English monarchy, America has become a nation of "kings". In Jasper, Texas, a few weeks ago (February 25, 1999), John William King, a White man, was sentenced to death for kidnapping a Black man, James Byrd, and dragging him along the road by a pick-up truck for three miles to his death. Several years ago, an African American who had sustained a brutal beating from some police officers became a national figure, but not necessarily a national hero. His name was Rodney King. His famous question in the aftermath of the legal saga, which followed his tragic experience, was simply this: "Can we all get along?"

Several years before Rodney, there was another man named King who was assassinated in Memphis in April 1968. Who assassinated him, and why, has still not been fully determined? But it was not his death that mattered so much as the moral legacy and prophetic quality of his life. He proclaimed in his own inimitable way the dream that he had, that one day people would no longer be judged by the color of their skin but by the content of their character. His name was not Rodney but Martin, but he was still a "King" nevertheless. If Rodney King asked the multiculturalist question, then Martin Luther King Jr. proclaimed the transculturalist vision.

But there is another King who was put to death because he behaved more like an outsider in his own culture. He came to his own people, and his own people did not receive him. He was a multicultural misfit. He came not to be served but to serve. He was not a "King" but the King of Kings. He did not have a dream. He had a mission. His mission was to draw every person into the Kingdom of God. For him, the Cross was the supreme center of integration and liberation, the point where cultures did not matter in the end. For transculturalism is taken up into resurrection, and neither circumcision matters anything nor uncircumcision, but a new creation. For, God is always in Christ reconciling the whole world to Godself. This is not myth. This is fact. This is faith. This is life. AMEN

FROM CONVERSION TO TRANSFORMATION: THE LIFE AND THOUGHTS OF ROMNEY MOSELEY

T his is for me a very proud and privileged moment, as I share in this historic occasion of the inauguration of the Romney Moseley Memorial Lecture Series, here at Trinity College, Toronto. I am very grateful to the organizers of this new series, to Dean Donald Wiebe and the Divinity Faculty, to The Reverend Stephen Fields and his colleagues, and the Diocese of Toronto, for their decision to launch this series in fitting memory of this notable, yet modest, Christian scholar and leader in the Church. I consider this exercise on my part as a continuing effort to repay the debt that I owe to him, as I shall shortly explain.

With the publication of his book *Becoming A Self Before God*, in the Spring of 1991, Romney Moseley obviously had no idea that it would be his first and only monograph. His autograph in my copy read thus: *"To Kortright, A faithful friend, brother, and counselor, An inspiration for critical transformations in my life. With abiding gratitude and affection, Romney."* We had first met in Barbados in 1980 while I was serving as Rector of his home church and holding a joint appointment on the faculty of Codrington College. Our collaboration involved many facets, including preparation for, and officiating at, his marriage to Joan Maynard. I was also instrumental in helping to sponsor him for admission into Anglican Holy Orders by the Bishop of Barbados.

In his turn, Romney Moseley played a major role in helping to open doors for me in North America. He sponsored my participation at an important theological conference in Atlanta in 1980. This was followed by my further participation at a conference of theologians here at the Toronto School of Theology in 1981. It was here at this conference that I met the Dean of Howard University Divinity School, who invited me to consider joining his faculty as a senior professor of theology. I eventually decided to accept the appointment at Howard; and I have never regretted that decision.

Along the way, Romney and I often pushed each other to think again, to produce, to publish, to prepare the way for others, to point others to opportunities for advancement. We were determined to sharpen the meaning of Caribbean independence, to challenge ecclesiastical and academic establishments towards greater compassion on the one hand, and more effective service on the other. It is therefore my great joy to share with you some of my reflections on his life and thought, and to suggest in some small way what are the lasting values of his religious and intellectual legacy. I have chosen to use two of his signature words: "From Conversion To Transformation".

Romney McIvor Samuel Moseley was born in Barbados, West Indies, on September 25, 1943. He grew up in the parish of Christ Church as a normal, well-rounded, Caribbean boy. He enjoyed almost all of the rights and privileges of Caribbean ecological, sociological, and institutional life. Church, school, family, sports, beaches, girlfriends, and various forms of cultural creativity all played a significant part in his human development. After receiving his early education in Barbados at the leading Secondary School for Boys (Harrison College), he proceeded to Boston University from where he graduated as a biology major in 1968. He always wanted to be a priest, but his elders are said to have preferred him to become a medical doctor. Romney, however, chose eventually to study religion.

From Boston, he entered Harvard Divinity School where he graduated with the B.D. (<u>Magna cum laude</u>) in 1971. He followed this up seven years later with his Ph.D. in Religion and Society, also from Harvard. The title of his doctoral dissertation was: "Religious Conversion: A Structural -Developmental Analysis". It was the professional and vocational working out of the broader implications and contradictions of that work at Harvard, under such people like James Fowler, William Rogers, and H. Richard Niebuhr, that was to occupy the rest of his professional and intellectual life. His sojourn at Harvard was filled with many exciting and enriching experiences. He served as a Teaching Fellow in Afro-American studies, in Religion and Identity, and as a Senior Research Associate. His major appointments were first at the University of Virginia (1975 - 80). During that period, he also did brief stints at Hollins College in 1979, and the University of St. Thomas, Houston, Texas, in 1980. He spent one year at the Interdenominational Theological Center in Atlanta as Assistant Professor of Ethics (1980 - 81), where he taught courses in Black Church Studies and Social Ethics, and Moral Reasoning.

His longest stay was at the Candler School of Theology at Emory University (1981 - 89). There he served in various capacities ranging from Associate Director for the Center For Faith Development, Associate Dean for Academic Affairs, Associate Professor of Theology and Human Development, to Chairman of the Graduate Department of Religion and Personality. He also directed the Master of Theology program, and the joint degree programs in Law and Theology, and Business in Theology for three years. Here at Trinity College, Toronto, (1989 - 1992), Romney served as Associate Professor of Divinity. His courses were mainly in the area of Ethics and Society. During his last year here, he offered courses with such titles as: "Suffering, Evil and the God of Love", "Congregations: Theological Ethics and Social Analysis", "Virtues and Vices", and "Faith And Ethics".

Most of his teaching, research, writing, and presentations were in the area of Theology and Human Development, and he contributed several chapters, articles, and reviews relating to faith-development and religious transformation. It was within the contours of these basic concerns that he pursued three fundamental issues: the evolution of his own personal story, the challenges of pastoral theology, and the imperatives for the Christian ethic. Princeton Theological Seminary was to have provided him with a fresh home-base to further pursue these issues more extensively and creatively. He was preparing to move to Princeton as Professor of Ethics in 1992, when his brilliant career was ended by his untimely death.

In addition to being a scholar of considerable repute and outstanding characteristics, Romney Moseley always took his sense of vocation to the sacred priesthood very seriously. He enjoyed the rites and ceremonies of Ecclesia Anglicana, especially whenever he made his return visits to the Caribbean. The life of the priest was intricately and intimately woven into the very fabric of Romney's spiritual, moral, and professional life. His untiring efforts to offer compassionate guidance, pastoral care and counseling, professional insights to fellow priests, and theological leadership in critical areas of discernment, were all part of the ministry in which his soul would often delight.

The Intellectual Pilgrimage

Romney Moseley was thrust into the harsh realities of a socio-psychological and vocational dilemma as he struggled for educational and professional advancement from Boston to Cambridge, from Charlottesville to Atlanta, and finally here in Toronto. He explained the reason for his sojourn in North America with these words: "Despite being victimized by racism, we sought to achieve the best that America could offer. Moving on up in the Caribbean means moving on out. Most of us came here to improve our professional status and we gained more than we lost."[1] His main forte was in the field of developmental psychology. On two different occasions in the early 1980's, he visited my Philosophy of Religion classes at Codrington Theological College, Barbados, to deliver lectures on William James. Now James had been a Harvard man, and so was Romney. But James was not a Caribbean man, and so unlike Romney. Romney's dilemma was to live in the world of the Harvard-oriented fields of concern with human developmental behaviors, while holding fast to his obligations of interpreting Caribbean livelihood and human dignity, in the face of massive forces of oppression and systemic injustice.

Could he sustain both interests? Could he increase in wisdom and stature as a scholar, and in favor with his colleagues in the field of developmental theories of religious behavior, and at the same time enhance his reputation and usefulness as a Caribbean scholar, ideologically located in the underside of history? Could he coordinate a fruitful conversation between these two worlds? His writings suggest that he struggled to give it his best shot. But he found great difficulty in submerging his existential struggles, as he wrestled with the current theories of his guild. He often attempted to integrate both trends. Sometimes it worked, sometimes it did not.

In his essay entitled "Faith Development and Conversion in the Catechumenate" (1984), he began by defining faith as "the activity of surrendering one's self totally to an ultimate and transcendent source of meaning and power." "In religious terms", he said, "the heart is given completely to God."[2] This definitional approach to faith was to become a basic theme of his thinking later, as he struggled with the meaning of *kenosis* as a dominant factor involved in human transformation. Here however, he was already taking issue with his colleague and mentor, James Fowler, and his famous theories about the six stages of faith development. Moseley was already becoming very uneasy about the very formulae with which he had worked for several years as Fowler's colleague. He explained that Fowler's stages-of-faith theory was based on a principle of cognitive equilibrium, with the assumption that one can achieve increasingly higher levels of development in one's faith journey. He referred to it as an "ambiguous mixture of Piagetian cognitive-structuralism, Erikson's passion for the intrinsic wholeness of the person, and Loevinger's argument in favor of a principle of coherence underlying ego development."[3]

Romney leaned more to the pragmatism he had found in William James and Bernard Lonergan. He thought that while Bernard Lonergan's typology of three types of conversion – intellectual, moral, and religious - differed from Fowler's stages of faith theories, it added something which Fowler's seemed to lack. For while Fowler concentrated on the psychological development of faith, Moseley was passionately concerned with the issue of what he called "ultimate faith". He said that ultimate faith "haunts us, particularly when faith development is misconstrued as a 'hothouse' for accelerating the production of faith."[4]

It must be clearly noted, however, that Moseley was not yet about to abandon the "stages-of-faith" school entirely, for he was still working very closely as Fowler's associate at Emory. He was simply wrestling with the issue of conversion as it made its way through the presumed stages of development. "Locked in a tunnel vision of linear progression and hierarchical stages, the moral life and religious faith fall victim to progressivism and triumphalism," he wrote. "Triumphalist ideologies ignore the history of suffering and eschatological hope for divine justice and freedom maintained by victims of oppression."[5]

Nevertheless, he loved such words as *telos, eschaton, praxis, metanoia, covenant,* and he wanted faith to be answerable to these key concepts in the religious discourse. Lonergan thus helped him to revisit Fowler's hold on him. He wrote: "This description (Fowler's Stage Five) needs to be supplemented by a view of religious conversion as the ultimate transformation of the self through faith. Lonergan's view of religious conversion as a falling in love with God not only adds to developmental stages a notion of sublation but, more importantly, reaffirms St. Paul's conviction that integral to the development of faith is the development of love and hope for an age to come."[6] Romney was already moving away from the position he had shared with Fowler three years earlier when they both wrote of faith as a dynamic relationship of trust and loyalty to centers of value, to an "operative image of power", and to "a master narrative" in our lives.[7]

Romney found it increasingly difficult to deal with faith as "the structuring of meaning", as Fowler had been propounding. He said that "faith is always more than its empirical stages. This 'more than' quality, the 'surplus of meaning', has to do with the paradox of seeking the eternal in the temporal."[8] He wanted to preserve an "ontology of communion" between God and creation, but he found that such was lost in the organic metaphor of structural stages. He wanted to develop a theological anthropology which could be sustained on an entirely different axis, and which was more faithful to the real experiences and aspirations of human life as he knew it.

Listen to him as he tried to deal with the American cultural context: *"In a culture that thrives on superficial expressions of community and Christian solidarity which avoid fundamental issues of injustice and oppression, a theological anthropology that emulates triumph over suffering and collapses the tension of paradox will be found rather attractive, as will developmental theories that offer an idealized vision of human fulfillment. The irony is that this culture will never escape the painful paradoxes that permeate its testimonies of freedom, equality, and receptivity to the poor and oppressed. It cannot escape the pain of God. Developmental theories which reinforce progressivism at the expense of human suffering need to be challenged by a kenotic theological anthropology that reaffirms the pain of God in the person of Jesus Christ."*[9]

There were perhaps three factors that weighed heavily on Romney's theological and spiritual development. First, his Harvard research concerns were fast becoming uprooted. Two, his increased consciousness of being an Afro-Caribbean person increasingly urged him to identify more with the cries of their suffering and oppression in the face of American triumphalism. Three, his own personal medical condition must have made him more aware, by stages of his own suffering, of the paradox of the pain of God. For Romney, God was no God unless God both understood his suffering and suffered with him. This grounding of his theological anthropology was being nurtured by his own existential narrative. "It is impossible to find oral and religious meaning in our lives", he wrote, "without deliberately seeking the recovery of wholeness."[10]

In his preface to his book *Becoming A Self Before God*, he shared with us these very moving words: *"This book bears the marks of profound changes in the dialectic of struggle and surrender in my own life. In bringing it to completion, I came to appreciate, more and more, loved ones who created a space for me to recover a self that was in danger of being utterly consumed by a spiraling vortex of apocalyptic confusion. Not least among these loved ones are my wife, Joan Miriam, and daughter Julia Marisa."*[11]

It must never be forgotten, however, that the person who had made a profound impact on Moseley's intellectual development and pattern of interpretation was the nineteenth century Danish philosopher Soren Kierkegaard (1813 – 1855). Without attempting to draw any parallels between Moseley and Kierkegaard, it must be noted that they were both very bright, and both died very young (Kierkegaard at forty-two, and Moseley at forty-eight). Moseley himself wrote: "A major figure in my work is the Danish Lutheran theologian and philosopher, Soren Kierkegaard."

Kierkegaard was to become known as the father of existentialism. During his very creative and productive personal journey, he was constantly overwhelmed by the confrontation we face with the threat of death, the vastness of the universe, and the apparent meaninglessness of our brief life here on this earth. He had devoted most of his intellectual energies against the established Lutheranism of his day, the bourgeois culture that nurtured it, and the Idealism of the German philosopher Georg Hegel (1770 – 1831) which placed the highest possible premium on the role of reason. Hegel insisted that faith was not independent from reason. For Kierkegaard, two principles were paramount, the subjectivity or inwardness of truth on the one hand, and the irrational 'leap of faith' on the other. Kierkegaard preferred to speak of an "objective uncertainty". "Without risk," he wrote, "there is no faith. Faith is precisely the contradiction between the infinite passion of the individual's inwardness and the objective uncertainty. If I am capable of grasping God objectively, I do not believe, but precisely because I cannot do this I must believe. If I wish to preserve myself in faith, I must constantly be intent upon holding fast the objective uncertainty, so as to remain out upon the deep, over seventy thousand fathoms of water, still preserving my faith."[12]

Could anything good come out of the academy? Could the academy generate a set of religious theories to confront, rather than give sanction to, the rabid materialistic culture in North America? Romney would have replied: *"My theological sensibilities lead me to conclude that the salvation of the world is an 'in spite of' experience rather than a cooperative divine-human venture. The kernel of grace is the enduring reality of God's love despite human sinfulness and the frailty of our efforts to love God."*[13]

Did the voices of the oppressed peoples have anything significant to contribute to the debate about faith and its development? Romney said yes, for they were the voices that called "for changes in theological discourse to accommodate experiences of injustice and oppression of women and nonWhites from the so-called third world. These voices rail against the partialization of the Imago Dei by those who are bent on preserving an intransigent patriarchy and a sexist and racist fragmentation of the human community. There are also those countless souls broken by economic and political oppression."[14]

So, where did he himself fit in with this whole movement of faith development? Romney was emphatic about his position: "I am particularly concerned about the linking of faith and development. As a product of the African diaspora, I am suspicious of developmental models that relegate the experiences of so-called Third World persons to the lowest levels of human development. The idea that faith has anything to do with progress is an anathema to those who suffer in the bowels of personal or social oppression. However, if the goals of development truly reflect the hard paradoxes of faith, then it is appropriate to speak of faith development."[15]

What were these paradoxes? They were power and powerlessness, fulfillment and emptiness, guilt and forgiveness, brokenness and wholeness, sin and salvation. Thus, Romney could no longer focus on psychological formation without personal transformation, on theoretical assumptions without an emancipatory praxis embodying freedom, justice and love. It was this intellectual and personal struggle that led him inexorably to posit a "kenotic theological anthropology (which) casts the divine -human relationship in terms of the paradox of God's self-emptying and our empowerment to become what God intends us to be.

The self imagines its freedom to change and to grow only in relation to the One who gave freely of himself on the cross."[16] Romney's *theologia gloriae* was being radically replaced by his *theologia crucis*. *Kenosis* was fast becoming the central meaning of his personal pilgrimage. He understood more and more what it really meant to be on the underside of history, and all this combined to bring out the other side of Romney's existence - he was a Caribbean scholar who had to speak for, about, and to the Caribbean.

The Afro-Caribbean And His Critical Engagement

Moseley's sojourn in Atlanta enabled him to become engaged in a further extension of his major work on faith and its implications for the people of color. He had spent a year at the Inter-denominational Theological Center (ITC), a predominantly black seminary that served mainly the black churches in America. This brief stint at the ITC provided for him an invaluable opportunity in beginning to appropriate his theological and psychological ideas to the distinctive culture of the Black Church. In this regard, he could bring his own brand of blackness to interface directly and creatively with the African-American academic culture. It was here that he began to study the impact of the leadership in the Black Church and the ingredients necessary to strengthen the legacy of the Civil Rights movement, to further the gains already made by African Americans in their struggle for justice, freedom, and wholeness.

In a paper delivered in 1986, Moseley argued that the Black Church had been frustrated by "accommodationist and transactional leadership as it confronts the harsh realities of poverty racism, unemployment, etc." Following the thoughts of James Burns, he called for a development of "transforming leadership" in the Black Church. According to Burns, such leadership occurs "when one or more persons engage with others in such a way that leaders and followers raise one another to higher levels in motivations and morality."[17]

Turning later to the Caribbean, Romney Moseley recognized with other Caribbean theologians that the "core of the Christian gospel is freedom from all forms of oppression."[18] "We in the Caribbean are fellow pilgrims in the tradition and hope of the black church," he wrote, "... We loathe our dictators, but we are aware that their survival is due not to their dictatorial ingenuity but to our collective parasitic dependence on the hegemony of the superpowers."[19] Romney knew that the Caribbean struggle for freedom had to be waged on a number of fronts at the same time, internally and externally. It meant even freedom from the missionaries. Listen to him yet again: "Denominations which specialize in sending missionaries to the Third World are the very denominations that have been nurtured in the cradle of racism and imperialistic triumphal religion. They selectively use biblical literalism to cast out demons from the illiterate masses while they allow themselves to wallow in self-righteousness and privatized religion."[20] Romney knew the answer to the question: freedom from what? He was not clear on the answer to the question: freedom from where? He would not have found an easy answer if he treated freedom merely as a theological metaphor.

Freedom is beyond definition and control, beyond the reach of metaphor. I have maintained elsewhere that freedom is not merely the nature of God, and the will of God, it is also the gift of God. "Human freedom subsists in the continuing affirmation of divine freedom, and in the human response to the perceived call from God to be free.... the only freedom deep enough to offer and inspire emancipation, and authentic enough to be concretely functional, is essentially that which acknowledges its origins in the sovereign free God."[21] The Caribbean poor and powerless people know of a freedom in the midst of their condition which the rich and the powerful can neither discern nor understand. It is a subterranean freedom that God creatively nurtured in the context of slavery, indentureship, and colonialism. Where does freedom come from? My answer is: "Human freedom sings what Divine Freedom brings."[22]

Romney insisted that an appropriate theology of freedom for the Caribbean should be one of decolonization. Such a theology should not "incorporate the triumphal myths and metaphors of modernity". He wanted a Caribbean history that was shaped by an emancipatory Christology which would "come to terms with the fact that Christians cannot escape the paradox of suffering and liberation in salvation history."[23] Yet it was not just the Caribbean that Romney wished to take *kenoticism* seriously, that is, the spirituality and ethic of self-emptying. He felt that *kenoticism* had the power to effect the religious transformation of persons and the world. He saw it as the chief antidote to triumphalism, especially as we had now reached "a watershed in history when we must re-image the Incarnation in the light of God's compassion, literally, God's 'suffering with' humanity."

For him, poverty and suffering were the locus for establishing the truth of God's emancipatory praxis. In a very moving sentence, Romney declared that "the hardest part of living contemporaneously with Christ is to let God's self-emptying love in Christ become for us a way of loving God and one another."[24] How would we work out a kenotic emancipatory praxis? We would do so through obedience to God, by being led by God's Spirit in self-emptying love, and by exercising power through compassionate love. It thus becomes a mutual *kenosis*, says Romney, and that is "the heart of a people called by God to form genuine and covenantal relationships in a fragmented world."[25]

Romney's vision for a new Caribbean society moved him to suggest that "after years of colonialism and dependence, the people of the Caribbean deserve to be political and economic partners with the modern industrialized nations."[26] To my mind, that was merely a pipe dream from Toronto, where he wrote this. But it was an impossible dream in Bridgetown, Kingston, or Georgetown, where they knew exactly who they were dealing with. Caribbean people have come to realize that there can be no genuine partnership between the rich and the poor. They even quake under the rigors of the partnership between the rich and the rich. My experience has led me to recognize that the rich would never do anything that diminished the advancement of their own self-interests, whether in commerce, philanthropy, government, academia, or the church. Poor people survive despite the rich, not because of their help. Any theological construction for Caribbean freedom must take this fully into account.

Thus, it seems to me that for Caribbean people, far from looking for partnership with the rich, which is a virtual impossibility between unequals, they must struggle to radically pursue some fundamental biblical-theological models for freedom. Creativity must overcome Complacency. Covenant with God must neutralize Contempt for God's ordinary people. Communitarian compassion must eliminate Competitive individualism. Persistent Conversion, as that constant turning towards God's freedom in Christ, must overwhelm the insatiable desires for Conquest. The practical vision of God's final transformation of all things must forever confront the pervasive appetites to consume everything now.

Conclusion

T hroughout his scholarly life, Romney Moseley attempted to call us back again and again to a Christian way of life that was guided by what he called a "covenantal ethic of responsibility". It was a fundamental theme of a covenantal relationship between God and God's people. Jesus Christ, as Supreme Liberator, was also the mediator of that Covenant. For Romney, as indeed for all Christians, five things are clear about the God of Jesus Christ: *God is. God acts. God cares and suffers. God saves. God alone is God.* It is the knowledge of this that brings grace, and grace is the bearer of freedom, even in the midst of poverty, and injustice, and marginalization. God's grace has sustained our people, Romney's and mine, despite the other ungracious acts by which their existence has often been surrounded. Romney's greatest contribution to the social discourse in Canada was his seminal work on Christian ministry in a multicultural society. The report that bears his name *No Longer Strangers* was published after his death.

Suffice it to say currently, therefore, that the Caribbean understanding of divine grace does not necessarily translate itself into the ease of life, or into any escape from the harshness of our material existence. Yet it enables Caribbean people to be warm, gracious, generous, forgiving, tolerant, kind, friendly, and hospitable. All of these were qualities richly embodied in the life and person of Romney Moseley. The fact of human grace reflects the human understanding of divine grace. To that extent, Caribbean people have managed to maintain what can only be called a very gracious, if not always a graceful, society. This was the society from which Romney Moseley emerged, and to which he finally returned and was laid to rest.

In the very last address which I heard him deliver, Romney had this to say: "Witnessing to Christ's presence in our time means finding ways to make the love of Christ work in a world fragmented by tribalism, ethnocentrism, racism and other 'isms'. This brokenness of the world recapitulates the offense of the Cross but also the promise of new life in Christ. This dialectic of memory and hope informs our identity as a people of the African diaspora, a rainbow church whose strength, freedom and restoration come from the grace of God."[27]

In the St. Bartholomew's churchyard, Barbados, where his last remains are placed there is a headstone at his grave. That stone stands as a constant reminder, as it proudly proclaims, that Romney Samuel McIvor Moseley was a "Faithful Priest, Father, Husband, Scholar, Counsellor, Friend." It is also embellished with these words from a well-known hymn: *For Thy Dear Saint O Lord / Who strove in Thee to live / Who found in Thee a great reward / Our grateful hymn receive."* AMEN.

Endnotes

1 Romney Moseley, "Contempt Or Collegiality: Which Way Forward?" Caribbean Anglican Consultation II, Washington, D.C. 1991, (mimeo.), p.3

2 See Robert Duggan ed., <u>Conversion And The Catechumenate</u>, (Paulist, Ramsey, NJ., 1984), p.145

3 <u>Ibid.</u> *p. 151*

4 *<u>Ibid</u>. p. 156*

5 <u>Ibid.</u> p. 12

6 <u>Ibid.</u>, p.162

7 See Barbara Brown Taylor ed., <u>Ministry And Mission</u>, (Post Horn Press, Atlanta, 1985) p.73

8 Moseley, <u>Becoming A Self</u>, p.68

9 See Jack L. Seymour & Donald E. Miller ed., <u>Theological Approaches To Christian Education</u>, (), p.158

10 Moseley, <u>Becoming A Self</u>, p.76

11 <u>Ibid.</u> p.10

12 See Michael Peterson et. al. (ed.), <u>Philosophy Of Religion</u> (New York, Oxford, 1996), p.84

13 Romney Moseley, <u>Becoming A Self Before God</u>, (Abingdon, Nashville, 1991), pp.36-37

14 See Seymour & Miller ed., <u>op</u>. <u>cit</u>., p.157

15 Romney Moseley, <u>Becoming</u>, pp.40-41

16 See Seymour & Miller ed., <u>op</u>. <u>cit</u>., p.162

17 James M. Burns, <u>Leadership</u>, (New York, Harper, 1978) p.20

18 See Pobee, <u>op</u>. <u>cit</u>., p.109

19 See Barbara Brown Taylor ed., <u>op</u>. <u>cit</u>., p.26
20 <u>Ibid</u>., p.25
21 Kortright Davis, <u>Emancipation</u>, p.8
22 Kortright Davis, <u>Emancipation</u>, p.115
23 See Pobee ed., p.116
24 R. Moseley, <u>Becoming</u>, p.119
25 R. Moseley, <u>Becoming</u>, p.131
26 See <u>Toronto Journal</u>, (Fall 1990), p.241
27 Romney Moseley, "Collegiality..", p.11

About the Author

Kortright Davis is an Anglican priest who was born in Antigua, West Indies. He was trained for the Anglican priesthood at Codrington College in Barbados, where he was once called to serve as the first descendant of slaves to be the Principal (Ag.) of that College. He was one of the founding executives of the Caribbean Conference of Churches. He is Rector Emeritus of The Church of the Holy Comforter in the Episcopal Diocese of Washington DC, where he served for 27 years. Currently, he is Professor of Theology at the Howard University School of Divinity, and Commissary to two Anglican Dioceses in the Church in the Province of the West Indies (CPWI). He was formerly a member of the Anglican/Roman Catholic International Commission (ARCICII), and the Faith & Order Commission of the World Council of Churches, as well as the Inter-Anglican Doctrinal and Theological Commission. He holds degrees from the Universities of London, UWI, and Sussex, as well as honorary degrees from the General Theological Seminary, The Virginia Theological Seminary, and the University of the West Indies. Davis has published extensively in the areas of Theology, Ministry Studies, Caribbean History, and Emancipatory Religious issues. He and his wife Joan reside in Kensington Maryland and are the proud parents of three children and five grandchildren.

CPSIA information can be obtained
at www.ICGtesting.com
Printed in the USA
BVHW040223240321
603329BV00016B/810

9 780228 851141